Local
Multi-Use Trails

Agoura, Calabasas, Malibu, Moorpark, Newbury Park, Santa Rosa Valley, Simi Valley, Thousand Oaks, Topanga, West Hills, Westlake Village

www.MultiUseTrails.com

Disclaimer

Horseback riding, mountain biking, and hiking are potentially dangerous sports and the user of this book assumes responsibility for any risks that may occur. Please use common sense and good judgment when using the trails. The author and publisher have made every attempt to provide accurate and thorough information. There is a possibility for error. The accuracy cannot be guaranteed. Mileage and elevation are approximate and may differ from other sources. Technical and aerobic ability are estimated. Trails and terrain change over time. Trails may be closed at times due to unknown circumstances. The author and publisher are not responsible for getting lost, damage, mishap or injury caused by the trails listed in this book. It is understood that anyone attempting any of the trails is familiar with the potential risks involved in hiking, biking, and horseback riding, and the risks involved in using multi use trails. There are unknown elements such as wild animals, heat, lack of water, unknown weather, and poisonous plants on the trails. It is recommended to bring a topo map, water, food, hat, sunscreen, and a first aid kit with you.

Photographs by T.C. Badalato, Kelly Murphy, Darlene Goodman, and Jeannette Welling.

For trail updates and changes, please refer to our website.
website: http://www.multiusetrails.com

Edition 1.0

Printed in the United States of America.

Acknowledgments

Special thanks to T.C. Badalato with Nature Fine Art Photos, my wonderful boyfriend, for lugging his heavy camera gear on our bike rides, for his electronic knowledge with the GPS, computer, and all the necessary applications.

Special thanks to Drs. Barry and Bart Goodman with the Goodman Chiropractors in Thousand Oaks for helping fix my back allowing me to continue tracking mileage on the bike.

Special thanks to Gina Virzi Kelly and Alan Ver Chick for showing me the best Simi Valley trails.

Special thanks to Marty for returning my GPS that I lost on the trail.

Special thanks to Shelly Austin, COSCA Associate Planner; Bruce Pace, COSCA Head Park Ranger, for looking over the book and for adding new trails and maintaining our existing trails.

Special thanks to my riding companions for joining me and trusting me to take them on numerous explorations.

Special thanks to Gina Smurthwaite, a founding member and previous chairperson of COSTAC, a founder of COSF, a sponsor of the Glider Hill trail system as part of the COSF Adopt-a-Trail program, and a technical editor/writer, for taking the time to edit the book and for sponsoring our trails and open space.

Last but not least, special thanks to my two horses Walt and May for carrying me on the trails in the hot weather up and down the steep hills, and standing still so I can take pictures and write information down.

Table of Contents

Newbury Park

Thousand Oaks

Topanga

West Hills

Westlake Village

BEWARE: The MRCA has installed hidden cameras at the stop signs near the top of Reseda Blvd at the Marvin Braude Mulholland Gateway Park, the Top of Topanga Overlook, Franklin Canyon Park, and the Temescal Gateway Park. The fines for running the stop signs are $100-$175.

Safety

Trail safety should always be practiced. There is a possibility that rattlesnakes, mountain lions, bobcats, or other wild animals may be around. Bring a companion whenever possible. Although rattlesnakes are most prevalent during the hotter months and the longer daylight hours, they can be seen year round. Be extra cautious when the grass is high and the trail is narrow. Wearing boots and covering up the lower legs can be helpful. Ticks like moist cool temperatures. Try to avoid low hanging bushes and narrow trails during tick season. Always check your clothing after an outing on the trails. Poison oak is a plant that should be avoided. Some people are terribly reactive to poison oak, while others are not. We use the term "bunches of three, leave it be." Poison oak gets very colorful in the fall, otherwise the plant is a beautiful dark green with groups of three leaves and is usually found on the north-facing slopes.

Multi-Use Trails

Multi-use trails allow for hikers, runners, equestrians, and mountain bikers to enjoy trails together. Multi-use trails follow specific guidelines for new trails enabling safety for all such as: terrain, grade, vegetation width and height, tread, line of sight, bench construction, turn radius, passing sections, and more. Although there are specific guidelines, always use your best judgment when choosing which trail to use. Some trails may not be safe for all uses due to blind turns, drop offs, heavily traveled, overgrown trails, or too narrow for safe passage. I have ridden all of the trails mentioned in this book using my GPS and bike cyclometer when possible.

Trail Etiquette

We should all share the trails equally. Many people hike our trails; they may not be very sure-footed; if they get startled they may slip and fall. If trails become unsafe, they can become closed to the public.

Mountain bikers should be courteous to all users including other mountain bikers. The uphill rider has the right of way when passing. When riding in opposing directions, please follow the rules of the road and stay on the right. Bikers may carry bells to inform other trail users that they are approaching. The bells should be used in a polite manner, while still slowing down and stopping when necessary. Hikers seem to appreciate the bells which alert the hiker that a mountain biker is approaching. Horses ears are very sensitive. The bells may startle horses in which case the rider may ask for the bells to be turned off. Please be courteous. When standing aside waiting for the horse to pass, please do not hide behind a bush so the horse cannot see you – make yourself seen, try to keep still, and speak in a calm voice. Ask the rider which side of the trail you should stand on. If they don't hear you, stand on the downhill side. If you are using an umbrella and an equestrian is approaching, please turn your back to the horse and close the umbrella until the horse safely passes.

Always ride as if there is someone around the next turn. Brakes and reins should always work. Slow down for horses; the rider will let you know if its safe to pass. Slow down for other mountain bikers, hikers, parents with children, parents pushing strollers, also the elderly. Runners should slow down as well; don't try to run past a horse and squeeze in between a bush and an edge. Parents please don't allow your child to run towards a horse and try to pet it. Please ask first and, if given permission, walk towards the horse slowly with a quiet voice.

Please pick up after your dog. Dog walkers should leave the trails free of any debris. There are bags offered at many trailheads for debris removal.

Parking lots should be left free of debris including horse manure. Please do not take up more spaces than necessary and do not block any cars or horse trailers. Leave at least one car's length if parked behind or in front of a horse trailer. If parked in front of houses, please pick up debris and please keep the volume down.

Cheeseboro/Palo Comado Canyons

SNMRA
Mountains Recreation and Conservation Authority Parkland
Rancho Simi Recreation and Park District Open Space
Santa Monica Mountains Conservancy

Cheesebro and Palo Comado Canyons contain thousands of beautiful acres located in the northern section of the Santa Monica Mountains in the Simi Hills with miles of public trails. The area is filled with coastal sage scrub, chaparral, oak riparian woodlands, and grassy meadows. There is an expansive network of trails connecting to the adjacent open space areas including Upper Las Virgenes Open Space to the east, and Lang Ranch/Woodridge Open Space to the northeast. Cheeseboro Canyon Trail, the Palo Comado Canyon Trail, and Cheeseboro Ridge Trail are three of the main fire roads heading north that connect to a network of trails. Cheeseboro Canyon Trail runs through the center of the park along the valley floor. The trail starts as a wide flat trail for the first 3 miles, leading to a single track through Sulphur Springs climbing up a semi-technical trail leading to Sheperd's Flat. The beginning of the trail makes a great out-and-back easy ride with a rest spot at a picnic table shaded by oaks just before the trail narrows. Palo Comado Trail on the west end of the park begins as Chesebro Rd. dead ends. It extends for 3.7 miles beginning with a moderate climb gradually getting steeper towards the top leading to China Flat. The Cheeseboro Ridge Trail is a long steep climb accessed from Cheeseboro Canyon Trail. The trail skirts along the ridge climbing up and down the canyons for 7.8 miles reaching Albertson Mtwy.

The area can accommodate all levels of ability with wide flat trails, long tough hills, and fun technical single track trails. This area is very popular especially with mountain bikers, runners, hikers, and equestrians. Weekends and holidays can be very crowded. If you are horseback riding, your horse should be comfortable with bikes. If traveling by bicycle, please pass slowly allowing plenty of space between you and the other trail user. The area gets hot and dusty in the summer and there isn't any water available.

There are 3 areas for parking. Equestrian parking is at the Agoura Equestrian Center on the corner of Chesebro Rd/Driver Ave approximately one mile from the main parking area. The

Cheeseboro/Palo Comado Canyons

Cheeseboro Canyon Trail travels on both sides of Chesebro Rd heading north and connects with the main park after one mile. There is a lower parking lot on the corner of Chesebro Rd outside of the gates. The main parking lot is a right turn when you reach the small parking lot for .2 mile and can be filled by 9 am on the weekends. The parking lot is open from dawn to dusk. There are picnic tables and restrooms at the main trailhead. The trails can all be accessed from either of the parking lots.

Palo Comado Canyon Trail to Ranch Center Road

Highlights:	A lot of climbing up grassy hillsides with canyon views with firm footing; sandy patches
Miles:	8.7 miles
Elevation:	1200 ft
Estimated time:	biking: 1-1.5 hr
	hiking and horseback riding: 2-3 hrs
Technical:	★★ ☆ ☆ ☆
Aerobic:	★★★ ☆ ☆
Restrooms:	Cheeseboro parking lot
Water:	drinking fountain, automatic horse waterer at the equestrian parking lot
Dogs:	on leash
Parking:	parking lot is free

Directions to Trailhead: GPS 34.146179,-118.738657
Chesebro Rd, Agoura
101 Fwy: exit 35 Chesebro Rd. North on Palo Comado Cyn Rd. Right on Chesebro Rd. Equestrian parking is on the corner of Driver Ave and Chesebro Rd. Main parking lot is 1 mile on Chesebro Rd. Turn right at the small parking lot.
*Elevation and mileage are approximate.
Heavy mountain bike traffic on Cheeseboro Cyn Tr. This is a non-technical ride with firm smooth footing for most of the time. There are two steep hills leading to a a long flat section amongst the oak trees.

Palo Comado Canyon Trail to Ranch Center Road

Overview: Beginning at the equestrian parking lot, head north along Chesebro Rd on the left (west) side of the street. The single track parallels the street. There are a couple seasonal water crossings to go through that become sandy when dry. **(1)** After .8 mile the trail splits; cross Chesebro Rd **(2)** Continue on the trail along the fence that goes around the main parking lot .3 mile. **(3)** On the northwest side (left if back is to the restrooms) of the parking lot is Modelo Tr. Follow Modelo Tr north .5 mile. The trail is a continual climb heading north. **(4)** Left at the first junction .7 mile continuing uphill **(5)** Left at the next junction on the Palo Comado Connector ascending and descending 1 mile. **(6)** Right (north) at the Palo Comado Cyn Tr. 1.1 miles along the wide moderately flat trail. **(7)** Right on Ranch Center Rd as the trail ascends up a steep hill and descends down a steep hill 1.2 miles leading to Cheeseboro Canyon Tr. **(8)** Right on Cheeseboro Canyon Tr 2.1 miles. Cheeseboro Canyon Tr is a very popular trail. **(9)** Just before reaching the main

Cheeseboro Cyn Tr

Palo Comado Canyon Trail to Ranch Center Road

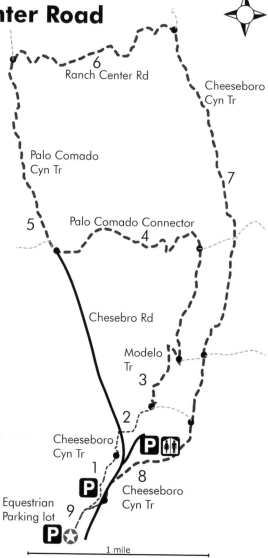

parking lot, Cheeseboro Canyon Tr branches to the left; continue .8 mile. The trail passes by an old wooden shed and corral and parallels Chesebro Rd. **(10)** At the next split, stay to the right heading towards the street, cross the street, turn left (south) and continue along the fence .2 mile back to the equestrian parking lot.

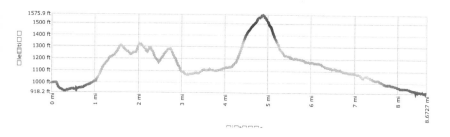

Cheeseboro Canyon Trail/ 🚴 🧗 🏇
Sulphur Springs

Highlights:	Scenic trail; mountain bikers favorite; some technical single track; sulfur springs
Miles:	9.3 miles
Elevation:	800 ft
Estimated time:	biking: 1-1.5 hrs hiking and horseback riding: 2-3 hrs
Technical:	★★★✦☆
Aerobic:	★★★☆☆
Restrooms:	Cheeseboro parking lot
Water:	no
Dogs:	on leash
Parking:	parking lot is free

Directions to Trailhead: GPS 34.15634,-118.731056
Chesebro Rd, Agoura
101 Fwy: exit 35 for Chesebro Rd. North on Palo Comado Cyn Rd. Right on Chesebro Rd. Main parking lot is 1 mile on Chesebro Rd. Right turn at the small parking lot.
*Elevation and mileage are approximate.

Overview: Heavy mountain bike traffic on Cheesboro Cyn Tr. Residential street riding on Chesebro Rd for one mile with Modelo Tr option instead of street travel. The footing is firm, smooth ground with loose rocky sections, climbing sandstone rocks with moderate hills. This is a popular trail for hikers, mountain bikers, and equestrians. The trail begins at the main parking area. **(1)** Pass the restrooms and head north along the moderately flat fire road 1.5 miles. **(2)** At the split in the trail stay to the left .9 mile leading to a single track. The groomed oak-shaded busy fire road turns to a single track passing through an underground sulfur spring. **(3)** The sulfur spring area is full of green vegetation for a short time. The trail travels along the valley floor on a groomed single track in between the canyon walls with abundant native vegetation and beautiful wildflowers in the spring 1.8 miles leading to Sheperd's Flat. The climb is gradual with two technical sections climbing up boulders. **(4)** At Sheperd's Flat, turn left (west) on Sheep Corral Tr .9 mile. Sheep Corral Tr is a single track with a moderate climb. This section of the trail can develop ruts after a heavy rain. Once the trail begins to descend before reaching

Cheeseboro Cyn Tr

Cheeseboro Canyon Trail/ Sulfur Springs

Palo Comado Fire Rd, there is a single track on the south (left) side of the trail. **(5)** Dead Cow Tr is a technical, rocky, rutted trail .7 miles long. There is an option to descend down Palo Comado instead of going down Dead Cow Tr. **(6)** Palo Comado intersects the trail, so continue down the hill (left turn) 2 miles. **(7)** The trail dead ends and turns into Chesebro Rd. To avoid the street, left on Palo Comado Connector Tr, right on Cheeseboro Cyn Tr. Follow Chesebro Rd 1.3 miles. **(8)** Left into the small parking lot and continue up the street .2 mile to the main parking area.

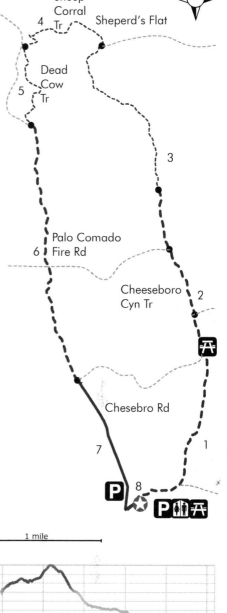

N

Sheep Corral Tr
4

Sheperd's Flat

Dead Cow Tr
5

3

Palo Comado Fire Rd
6

Cheeseboro Cyn Tr
2

Chesebro Rd

7

1

P
8

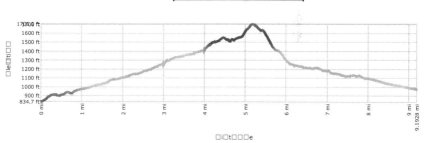

1 mile

Palo Comado Canyon Trail/ 🚴 🧗 🐎
Cheeseboro Ridge Trail Loop

Highlights:	A non-technical loop on fire roads; heavy climbing; panoramic views
Miles:	17.5 miles
Elevation:	3000 ft
Estimated time:	biking: 2.5-3 hrs
	hiking and horseback riding: 5-6 hrs
Technical:	★★ ☆ ☆ ☆
Aerobic:	★★★★ ☆
Restrooms:	Cheeseboro main parking lot
Water:	on leash
Dogs:	on leash
Parking:	parking lot is free

Directions to Trailhead: GPS 34.15634,-118.731056
Chesebro Rd, Agoura
101 Fwy: exit 35 Chesebro Rd. North on Palo Comado Cyn Rd. Right on Chesebro Rd. Main parking lot is 1 mile on Chesebro Rd. Right turn at the small parking lot.
*Elevation and mileage are approximate.

Overview: Heavy mountain bike traffic on Cheeseboro Cyn Tr. This is a non-technical trail mainly on fireroads with firm to rocky footing and a lot of climbing. This trail is tough on the legs, although the

Palo Comado Connector Tr

Palo Comado Canyon Trail/ Cheeseboro Ridge Trail Loop

views make it worth while. There isn't any water available on the trail, and there are times when the trail is far away from necessities. There are mountain bikes mainly on Palo Comado Cyn Tr, China Flat, and Cheeseboro Cyn Tr with a few bikes on the Albertson Mtwy and Cheeseboro Ridge Tr. The area can get very hot in the summer. Begin at the main parking lot. **(1)** Climb up the Modelo single track directly in front of the parking lot .5 mile, then left at the first intersection .7 mile. The trail is surrounded by beautiful grassy hillsides. **(2)** Left at the next junction on the Palo Comado Connector Tr 1 mile. The trail ascends and descends leading to Palo Comado Cyn Tr. **(3)** Head north (right) uphill 4 miles. Palo Comado Cyn Tr begins on the valley floor surrounded by an oak grove on one side of the trail and a hillside on the other. The fire road begins as a gradual climb and gets steeper as it nears China Flat. **(4)** Once the trail begins to gradually descend, you'll pass a single track on the right. At the next junction, turn right on the fire road. You'll ride through the partially shady flat oak grove .5 mile. This is a nice rest area before continuing on the Albertson Mtwy. You will pass single track trails spidering throughout; pass them and continue around a gate. **(5)** .1 mile after the gate, you'll come to a T in the road, stay right on Albertson Mtwy 1.9 miles. If you traveled to the left this would lead to Lang Ranch. While traveling along the mountain top, Albertson Mtwy offers almost 360 degree views. **(6)** Right turn at the next intersection down Cheeseboro Ridge Tr. The trail descends down the canyon traveling southeast following the contour of the mountain top. As the fire road drops back into the canyon, there are many hills with many climbs ascending back up the mountain to come down and right back up again 6.3 miles. **(7)** Right on Cheeseboro Ridge Connector Tr slight downhill .5 mile. **(8)** Left on Cheeseboro Canyon Tr descending slowly 2 miles back to the parking lot.

Palo Comado Canyon Trail/
Cheeseboro Ridge Trail

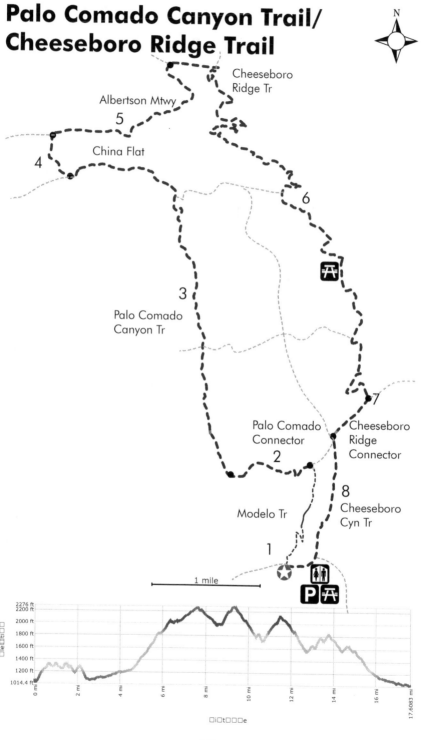

N

Cheeseboro
Ridge Tr

Albertson Mtwy

5

China Flat

4

6

3

Palo Comado
Canyon Tr

7

Palo Comado
Connector

Cheeseboro
Ridge
Connector

2

8

Modelo Tr

Cheeseboro
Cyn Tr

1

1 mile

Paramount Ranch

National Park Service
Santa Monica Mountains National Recreation Area

    Paramount Ranch is 2,700 acres of beautiful grassy rolling hills dotted with oak trees nestled in the Santa Monica Mountains. The ranch is adjacent to Malibu Creek State Park and the Ronald Reagan Ranch to the southeast across Mulholland Hwy. The year-round creeks carve through the ranch giving ample water for wildlife. There is an old western town still used for filming movies and taking photographs. Toward the front of the ranch, there is a flat area which used to be a racetrack and is now used for flying electric planes.

    Paramount is always a wonderful place to visit. There is ample free parking, restrooms, and a drinking fountain at the western town. With miles of trails to explore the area is great for a stroll or short hike. Horseback riding and hiking are common in the area. The temperature can get hot in the summer although there is some shade and year round creeks to cool off in.

Paramount Ranch

Paramount Ranch Loop

Highlights:	Beautiful grassy meadows with shaded oak trees, creeks, and an old western town
Miles:	2.3 miles
Elevation:	230 ft
Estimated time:	biking: 20 mins
	hiking and horseback riding: 1 hr
Technical:	★★ ☆ ☆ ☆
Aerobic:	★★ ☆ ☆ ☆
Restrooms:	yes
Water:	drinking fountain
Dogs:	on leash
Parking:	large parking area is free

Directions to Trailhead: GPS 34.117036,-118.754869
2903 Cornell Rd, Agoura Hills
101 Fwy: exit 36 Kanan Rd., north on Kanan Rd .3 mile, left turn on Cornell Way 2 miles. Paramount Ranch is on the right side of the street. If you pass Mulholland Hwy, you have passed the ranch.
Pacific Coast Highway: north on Malibu Cyn Rd 4.6 miles; continue onto Las Virgenes Rd. 1.7 miles. Left on Mulholland Hwy 3.2 miles. Right on Cornell Rd .2 mile. Left into the ranch.
*Elevation and mileage are approximate.

Overview: The hills are rolling and the footing is firm, smooth ground with a few rocks. The trail begins at the parking area near the restrooms. The ranch is a network of many short connecting trails. Each one is very beautiful. Some of these trails are not marked. The area is wide open and the connecting trails are visible most of the time. **(1)** This route travels south on the asphalt road .1 mile. **(2)** Make a right turn and cross over a cement bridge just before reaching the old western town. **(3)** After you pass through the town and picnic tables, follow the trail across the road from the old town. Hacienda Tr travels through the rolling grassy meadows spotted with oak trees. **(4)** You will come to a junction with a trail to the left leading to private property. Make a right onto Backdrop Tr. **(5)** Make a left on Bwana Tr and soon you're relaxing at the creek under the shade. There are rocks to cross the creek to avoid getting your shoes wet. **(6)** Right turn on Ebb Tide Tr. Just after the creek, the trail turns into a gravel road where you will pass by an old racetrack next to Cornel Rd. The racetrack is used for flying electric planes. **(7)** The

Paramount Ranch Loop

road will come to a fence. There is a trail to the right that goes around the gate and connects back to the gravel road. The gravel road will lead you back to the parking area.

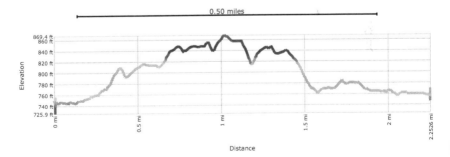

Malibu Creek State Park

Santa Monica Mountains National Recreation Area
California State Parks
Department of Parks and Recreation

Malibu Creek State Park consists of approximately 7,850 acres of rugged backcountry open space in the heart of the Santa Monica Mountains. Visitors can enjoy hiking, horseback riding, and mountain biking on over 40 miles of single track trails and fire roads. The fire roads are open to all uses; most of the single track trails are designated to specific uses. Hiking is allowed on all of the trails, horseback riding is allowed on most of the single track trails, and mountain biking is limited to a couple single trails within the park. A great amount of protected areas located within the Santa Monica Mountains border the park with trails connecting to other parks and open space including Paramount Ranch and Castro Crest.

Crags Road is the main trail of the park meandering along the valley floor from one end of the park to the other for approximately 3 miles with an elevation gain out and back of 400 ft. The footing is mainly flat and smooth. The first part of Crags Rd (approx. 1 mile) leads to the Rock Pool and Century Lake which are popular destinations for rock climbing, picnicking, and swimming. After a rain the trail can become very muddy. Just past the lake, after traveling through the dry creek bed full of oak trees and sycamore trees, you will come to the remains of the old MASH site. The Planet of the Apes and MASH were filmed at the park as well as many other television shows and movies. Just past the MASH site is the Bulldog Tr which is approximately 3.2 miles with an elevation gain of 1800 ft. leading to Castro Crest with beautiful views of sandstone peaks and 360 degrees of panoramic views. The park gets very crowded on holidays and weekends near the main attractions of the park. You will find many areas with shaded picnic tables. There are restrooms in both parking lots. The lower parking lot offers a drinking fountain and a vending machine. There are also porta potties near the visitor center off of Crags Road. The visitor center is approximately 1 mile west on Crags Road from the main entrance of the park. The main entrance is on Las Virgenes Rd. The cost of parking is $12, or a state park pass. There is a self-serve kiosk at the main entrance when attendants are unavailable.

Malibu Creek State Park

Hours are 8 am-10 pm. Street parking is available on sections of Mulholland Hwy near Grassland Tr and Cistern Tr. The Reagan Ranch on Cornell Rd at the west end of the park offers a small gravel parking lot with free parking. The Yearling Tr. leads from the Reagan Ranch to the main trails in the park which are for hiking and horseback riding only. Bikes are not allowed on the Yearling Tr. Dogs are not allowed on backcountry trails. There is parking at the Tapia Park parking lot off of Las Virgenes Rd about 1 mile past the main entrance. The parking lot is small. The cost of parking is $10 per vehicle

Equestrian parking is recommended at the main entrance and the Reagan Ranch. There is additional parking at Paramount Ranch, although to enter Malibu Creek State Park you have to cross Mulholland Hwy/Cornell Rd at the stop sign.

The Malibu Creek Family Campground offers drinking water, flush toilets, showers, 62 tent/RV spaces, tent spaces, dump station, fire rings, pets in campground for $35/night; call 800-444-7275 for reservations. The Malibu Creek Group Camp Walk-In for 10-60 people offers drinking water, flush toilets, showers, tent spaces, dump station, fire rings, pets in campground for $200/night call 800-444-7275.

MASH site

Bulldog to Tapia Park Loop 🚴 🥾 🐎

Highlights:	A climbers delight: panoramic views and sandstone peaks
Miles:	15.4 miles
Elevation:	2900 ft
Estimated time:	biking: 2.25+hrs
	hiking and horseback riding: 4+hrs
Technical:	★★★☆☆
Aerobic:	★★★★☆
Restrooms:	parking lot
Water:	drinking fountain in parking lot
Dogs:	no
Parking:	Main parking lot is $12
	Mulholland Hwy for cars is free

Directions to Trailhead: 34.103556,-118.713611
1925 Las Virgenes Rd, Calabasas
101 Fwy: exit las Virgenes Rd, south on Las Virgenes Rd 3 miles. RIght on Mulholland Hwy .1 mile. Trailhead is on the left.
PCH: north on Malibu Canyon Rd 4.5 miles; continue on Las Virgenes Rd 1 mile. Left on Mulholland Hwy .1 mile. Trailhead is on the left.
*Elevation and mileage are approximate.

Overview: Crags Rd can be crowded on the weekends and holidays. The terrain is varied—flat along Crags Rd, moderate along Mesa Peak Mtwy, and steep up Bulldog and down Backbone single track. The footing varies from embedded rocks along the dry creek bed to loose rocks up sections of Bulldog to firm smooth ground at times. You should be fit to do this loop. There isn't any water available. At mile 12.5 there is a creek crossing. The restrooms are not open at Tapia Park. Automobiles may park on Mulholland Hwy to utilize free limited street parking or in the state park for $12. Horse trailers should utilize the park's oversized parking stalls for a fee of $12 per vehicle or free with a park pass. **(1)** Begin on the Grassland Tr heading south towards Crags Road .5 mile. The trail branches down hill to the right. **(2)** Right on Crags Rd. After 1.7 miles, the trail narrows and becomes a dry creek bed .6 mile. Once you have reached the MASH site, Bulldog Mtwy. is on the left in approximately .3 mile. **(3)** Left (south) on Bulldog Mtwy. 3.2 miles with a 1,800 ft elevation gain. There are a few trails that branch off of the trail but are deadends. Poles are trail markers; there are also faded trail

Backbone Tr rock formation

Bulldog to Tapia Park Loop

signs to follow. At the top of Bulldog Mtwy there are incredible views surrounded by sandstone peaks. **(4)** Left down Castro Crest .8 mile to Corral Canyon Rd **(5)** Ride through the parking lot and continue on Corral Canyon Rd .3 mile to connect with the Backbone Tr **(6)** The Backbone Tr (Mesa Peak Mtwy) will be on the left side of the street with a trail going around a gate. It is a wide fire road with beautiful views 4.5 miles. Keep an eye out on the (north) left side of the trail for an interesting rock display. Continuing down the trail, it ascends up a couple short hills until the final long downhill. **(7)** Nearing the bottom of the fire road you will see a chain link fence on the left; start to keep an eye out for the Backbone single track on the right. It is steep, rocky, rutted and sometimes overgrown, but pretty. After .6 mile the trail ends at the Tapia Park parking lot on Las Virgenes Rd. This is where it can get tricky. Horses should travel through the creek crossing, but mountain bikers and hikers can do either the creek crossing or follow Las Virgenes Rd over the bridge with a very narrow shoulder. **(8) Creek Crossing**: From the bottom of the Backbone Trail there is a single track almost directly in front of the trail that parallels Las Virgenes for 50 ft. Cross the asphalt road; there will be a single track approximately 50-100 ft. to the left away from the street and around the gates. The trail descends to the creek crossing and continues for approximately 300 ft. The trail comes to a junction at the picnic benches and barbecues. Left on the trail. **(9) Street Crossing**: From the street at the Tapia Water Facility, ride along the highway over the bridge past Piuma Rd. .1 mile. Just after Piuma Rd there is a single track on the left; take the single track running parrallel to the asphalt road. This trail ends up at the picnic and barbeque area. Continue ahead on the trail. **(10)** Continue past the picnic benches and along a flat, shady trail around the gate .1 mile. **(11)** Continue .3 mile to the Tapia Spur single track. The trail is directly across the asphalt road. **(12)** Follow the trail 1.1 miles. It now has boulders in the middle of the trail to maneuver around. The trail comes out at the campgrounds. **(13)** Continue through the parking lot and along the gravel road .2 mile. **(14)** Left on the pavement for .1 mile coming out at the lower parking lot. **(15)** To continue on to Grassland Tr left on Crags Rd .3 mile, **(16)** right on Grassland Tr up and over the hill .6 mile to Mulholland Hwy.

Bulldog to Tapia Park Loop

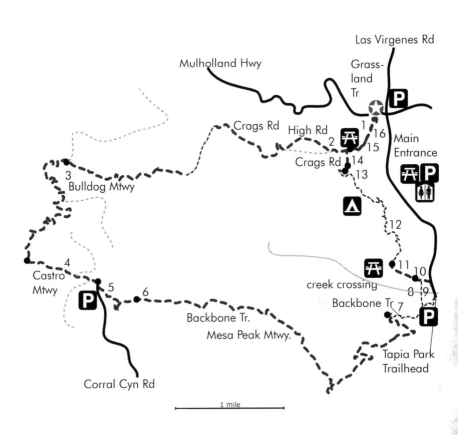

Las Virgenes Rd

Mulholland Hwy

Grass-
land
Tr

P

Crags Rd High Rd

1
16

Main
Entrance

2

15

Crags Rd

14

13

P

3

Bulldog Mtwy

12

4

Castro
Mtwy

11 10

creek crossing

8 9

5

6

Backbone Tr

7

P

Backbone Tr.

Mesa Peak Mtwy.

Tapia Park
Trailhead

Corral Cyn Rd

1 mile

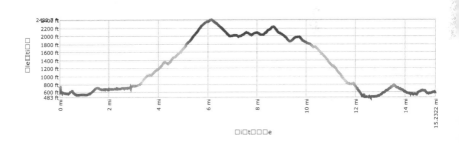

Phantom Trail Loop

Highlights:	A beautiful trail throughout Malibu Creek State Park offering panoramic views
Miles:	7.6 miles
Elevation:	1360 ft
Estimated time:	hiking and horseback riding: 2-3 hrs
Technical:	★★★✦ ☆
Aerobic:	★★★ ☆ ☆
Restrooms:	main parking area, visitors center
Water:	drinking fountain, vending machine
Dogs:	no
Parking:	main entrance $12 or CA state park pass

Directions to Trailhead: GPS 34.096756,-118.716588
1925 Las Virgenes Rd, Calabasas
101 fwy: exit 32 for Las Virgenes Rd toward Malibu Canyon, then south onto Las Virgenes Rd 3 miles. Destination is on the right.
Pacific Coast Hwy: north on Malibu Canyon Rd 4.5 miles. Continue on Las Virgenes Rd 1 mile. Destination is on the left.
*Elevation and mileage are approximate.

Overview: This loop crosses Mulholland Hwy twice. There is a walk along the dirt shoulder of Mulholland Hwy for approximately 200 ft from Cistern Tr to Phantom Tr. The hills are moderate with steep switchbacks. Footing is firm with sections of rocks.

View from the Phantom Tr

Phantom Trail Loop

Bikes are not allowed on Lookout Tr, Cistern Tr, and Phantom Tr. This trail begins at the lower parking lot in Malibu Creek State Park. **(1)** Travel west on Crags Rd. Cross over the wide cement bridge .4 mile. **(2)** The fire road will split. Follow High Rd to the right .5 mile climbing up and over a small hill. The fire road merges to the right back onto Crags Rd .4 mile to the Lookout Tr junction. **(3)** Right on Lookout Tr .4 mile. The Lookout single track climbs quickly leading to nice views of the park. The trail is narrow with a gradual drop on one side of the trail. **(4)** At the first junction right on Cistern Tr .3 mile. Cistern single track is steep with some rock stairs. The trail comes out on Mulholland Hwy. Many motorcycles ride on Mulholland Hwy. **(5)** Left (west) on Mulholland Hwy. The trail is not visible until approximately 200 ft. There is a wide shoulder to walk along before you cross the street. You should see the trail at this point. **(6)** Phantom Tr continues on the north side of the street. The single track is marked although the weeds can be high at times partially covering up the sign. Follow Phantom Tr 2.4 miles. Follow the trail signs the entire time. Alternate paths have been added to avoid some of the steep hills. The trail begins up switchbacks through a shaded area for a short time following along the ridgeline with 360 degree views. There are many sections of poison oak hanging into the trail. When the trail flattens out you are close to the junction. The trail is mostly flat for the entire trip back. **(7)** Right on the fire road .3 mile. This fire road leads to private property. Please follow the trail signs. **(8)** There is a single track on the left that leads through the seasonal creek for approximately 300 ft connecting to Liberty Cyn Fire Rd. **(9)** Right on Liberty Cyn Fire Rd 1 mile. You will pass Talepop Tr. **(10)** Sharp right turn at the next junction onto N. Grassland Tr .4 mile. You will cross a wooden bridge with rails on the sides. **(11)** The trail will come to a power station on an asphalt road. Right turn on the asphalt road for approximately 30 ft. Make a left after the power station connecting back onto the trail .3 mile leading to Mulholland Hwy. **(12)** Cross Mulholland Hwy. The trail continues across the street approximately 25 ft west on Mulholland Hwy. It is visible from the trail. Follow Grassland Tr .8 mile climbing up and over a small hill leading to Crags Rd. **(13)** Left on Crags Rd .2 mile to the parking lot.

Phantom Trail Loop

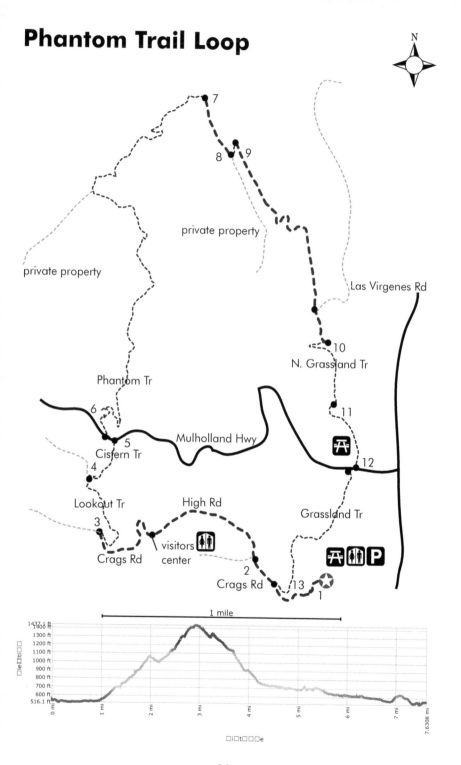

Talepop Trail Loop

Highlights: A stroll through a meadow climbing to views
Miles: 4.8 miles
Elevation: 400 ft
Estimated time: hiking and horseback riding: 1.5+ hrs
Technical: ★★✦☆☆
Aerobic: ★★☆☆☆
Restrooms: yes
Water: drinking fountain and vending machines
Dogs: no
Parking: Malibu Creek State Park $12 or state park pass

Directions to Trailhead: GPS 34.103556,-118.713611
Mulholland Hwy/Las Virgenes Rd, Calabasas
101 Fwy: exit 32 for Las Virgenes Rd toward Malibu Canyon. South onto Las Virgenes Rd 3 miles. Right on Mulholland Hwy .1 mile. Trailhead is on the right.
Pacific Coast Hwy: north on Malibu Canyon Rd 4.5 miles; continue on Las Virgenes Rd 1 mile. Left on Mulholland Hwy .1 mile. Trailhead is on the right.
*Elevation and mileage are approximate.
Overview: The route is flat with a mild climb. The footing is firm and smooth with patches of a few rocks. Bikes are allowed on the beginning of the ride on Grassland Tr; bikes are not allowed on Talepop Tr. The route begins in Malibu Creek State Park off of Mulholland Hwy. There is a very narrow shoulder when parking on the street, trucks with horse trailers should begin at the main entrance of the park with an extra mile of travel each direction.
From main entrance: follow Crags Rd .2 mile. Right turn on Grassland Tr .8 mile to Mulholland Hwy. Cross Mulholland Hwy and the trailhead is approximately 100 ft to the right (east). The trailhead is .1 mile west from Las Virgenes Rd on the north side of the street. **(1)** North on Grassland Tr away from the main park entrance, paralleling Las Virgenes Rd .3 mile. Grassland Tr has a nice flat to moderate grade. **(2)** Right turn around the power station on asphalt to connect back on the trail. The trail bends around to the right, crosses a bridge and comes to an intersection .5 mile. There is private property alongside the trail; please follow the trail signs. **(3)** Follow N Grassland Tr to the right 1.2 miles. There is a single

View from the Talepop Tr

Talepop Trail Loop

track (sometimes overgrown) to the left just before the bridge leading to Anza Park. **(4)** Follow the single track 1.8 miles climbing up and over the hill. When you reach the summit, there are panoramic views of Calabasas. The trail skirts along the ridge line for a short time before descending down to Liberty Cyn Fire Rd. **(5)** Left on Liberty Cyn Fire Rd .2 mile until reaching the next junction. **(6)** Right on N. Grassland Tr .4 mile crossing back over the wooden bridge. You are now retracing your steps on a portion of the return trip. **(7)** Go around the power station and make a left after the asphalt and continue .3 mile to Mulholland Hwy.

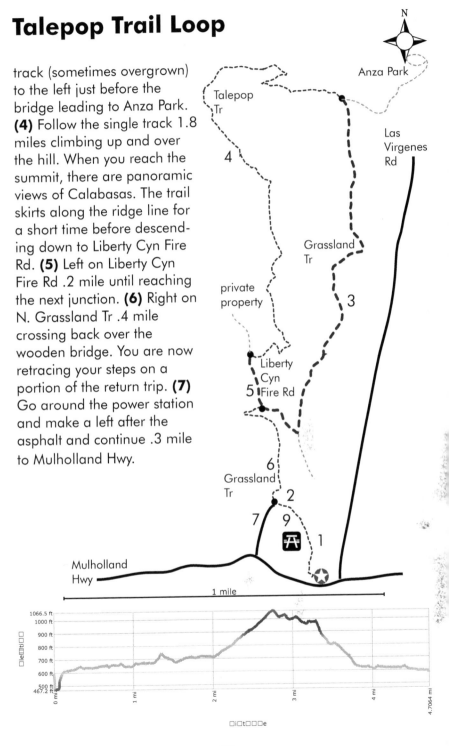

33

Malibou Lake Loop

Highlights: A shady trail through the forest leading to an overlook of Malibou Lake
Miles: 1.9 miles
Elevation: 400 ft
Estimated time: hiking and horseback riding: 45 mins-1 hr
Technical: ★★★☆☆
Aerobic: ★★☆☆☆
Restrooms: no
Water: no
Dogs: no
Parking: Ronald Reagan Ranch parking lot is free

Directions to Trailhead: GPS 34.112302,-118.750427
28754 Lake Vista Dr, Agoura
101 Fwy: exit 36 Kanan Rd. south (right) .4 mile. Left on Cornell Way 2.4 miles. Pass Mulholland Hwy. Left into the first driveway.
PCH: north on Kanan Dume Rd 6.2 miles. Slight right onto Mulholland Hwy 4.4 miles. Right on Lake Vista Dr 300 ft. Left into first driveway.
*Elevation and mileage are approximate.

Overview: Bikes are not allowed on this loop. The footing is firm ground with embedded rocks, loose and rutted in places from horse traffic. The grade is moderate. This loop can also be

View above Malibou Lake

Malibou Lake Loop

accessed from Paramount Ranch crossing Mulholland Hwy. Beginning at the Reagan Ranch Parking lot in Malibu Creek State Park **(1)** Walk along the flat trail that follows the driveway .4 mile leading to the ranch. **(2)** When the trail ends and the driveway veers to the right, stay straight onto the Yearling Tr .1 mile. **(3)** At the split, stay right going through the trees on the Deer Leg Tr .3 mile, there will be a picnic bench on the right under the shade. There aren't any trail signs. **(4)** Turn right up the Vista Lake Tr .7 mile up the shady trail. The trail gently winds up the hill. There is poison oak in places along the trail. Once you have reached the top with the lake in view, walk to the left for a few hundred feet for better views. **(5)** The return trip is down the fireroad to the right .4 mile back to the parking lot.

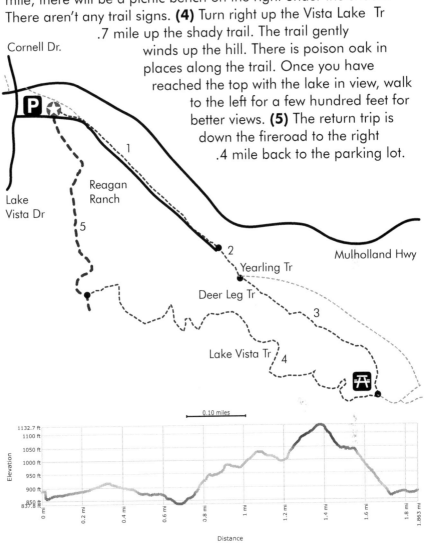

Calabasas/New Millenium Trail

City of Calabasas
Las Virgenes Municipal Water District
Mountains Recreation and Conservation Authority
Santa Monica Mountains National Conservancy Agency
Mountains Restoration Trust
Homeowners Associations in the City
Santa Monica Mountains National Recreation Area

Surrounded by miles of open space and park land, the Calabasas trail system is located within a rugged landscape in Calabasas with approximately 20 miles of multi-use trails. The area is located from the northeast intersection of Las Virgenes Rd and Mulholland Hwy running north paralleling Las Virgenes Rd to the 101 Freeway and extending to the east above Mulholland Hwy. With connecting trails leading to Cheeseboro and Palo Comado Canyon, Malibu Creek State Park, and the Upper Las Virgenes Canyon Open Space Preserve there are endless backcountry trails to explore.

The trails are mainly non-technical single track, although there are a couple newly developed trails that have very tight steep switchbacks with loose tread and full exposure on the edge of a hill. These sections are not recommended for horses and small children. The Millennium Loop Tr is the main trail that makes a loop traversing through the Oaks subdivision, ascending up and down canyons, passing through lush meadows, fragrant pine trees, grassy hillsides spotted with oak tress, and crossing wooden bridges. The trails range from open terrain to very tight switchback trails. The grade is moderate overall except for a few steep hills. The area is traveled mainly by hikers, dog walkers, mountain bikers, and a few equestrians. The area doesn't get very crowded.

Spring time is the most beautiful time of year with the tall green grass and wildflowers lining the trails, although the ticks are most prevalent during this time. If traveling by horseback, there can be soft spots in the ground after a rain. Allow time for the trails to dry to travel by horseback in this area.The best time to ride these trails is in the fall after the summer growth has been trimmed back. Trailheads for cars are at Bark Park, Juan Bautista De Anza West at the dirt parking lot next to the Mobil station .2 mile south of the 101 freeway, and the corner of Mulholland Hwy/Las Virgenes Rd.

Calabasas

Horse trailer parking is recommended at the Juan Bautista De Anza West at the dirt parking lot next to the Mobil station .2 mile south of the 101 freeway.

Bark Park Trail to Millenium Trail

Highlights:	95% single track with many switchbacks; scenic with views; climbs in and out of canyons
Miles:	13.6 mile loop
Elevation:	2600 ft
Estimated time:	biking: 2+hrs hiking and horseback riding: 4+hrs
Technical:	★★★✦☆
Aerobic:	★★★★☆
Restrooms:	porta potty
Water:	drinking fountain
Dogs:	on leash
Parking:	parking lot is free

Directions to Trailhead: GPS 34.133938,-118.702383
Bark Park Trailhead, 4232 Las Virgenes Rd, Calabasas
101 Fwy: exit 32 for Las Virgenes Rd toward Malibu Canyon. South onto Las Virgenes Rd 1 mile
Pacific Coast Hwy: South on Malibu Canyon Rd 4.6 miles; continue on Las Virgenes Rd 3.8 miles. It is on the right side of the street.
*Elevation and mileage are approximate.

Overview: The parking lot is small and crowded during weekdays. There are two sections of very steep switchbacks with a 50–ft drop. The Millenium Tr can be traveled in either direction, although the clockwise direction is recommended to travel downhill along the switchbacks. The trail is narrow and on the edge of a hill at times. There is a lot of climbing in and out of the canyons with a moderate grade, many switchbacks, some too tight to ride on a bike. The route begins at Bark Park dog park. **(1)** Continue up the pleasant Bark Park Tr 1.2 miles. **(2)** Turn left at the intersection on the Millenium Tr 2.9 miles. The trail drops down the

Bark Park Trail to Millenium Trail

canyon, crosses a muddy section, and skirts along the edge of a hillside. **(3)** At the next intersection, turn right on the gravel road .9 mile–Anza Loop Tr. **(4)** Pass the truck parking area for approximately 300 ft and continue on the trail to the left .8 mile to the next intersection. This turn is easy to miss. If you end up at the 101, you have gone too far. **(5)** Turn right at the intersection. The trail travels up and down switchbacks, through the canyon, crosses a bridge 1.4 miles. **(6)** Continue down the steep switchbacks leading to Parkway Calabasas .8 mile **(7)** Cross the street and connect to the trail directly across the street with switchbacks uphill .9 mile. **(8)** The trail levels off and rolls along the backside of houses on the west with beautiful views to the east through a few pine trees 1.3 miles to the ultimate view spot at to the top of the next set of steep switchbacks. **(9)** Continue down the steep switchbacks and along a narrow trail skirting the hillside that can get washed out. The trail continues down a canyon with a small water crossing and a dip that gets washed out 2.2 miles to an intersection. **(10)** Turn right at the intersection .8 mile to the Bark Park Tr. **(11)** Left down Bark Park Tr 1.2 miles.

View of the steep switchbacks

Bark Park Trail to Millenium Trail

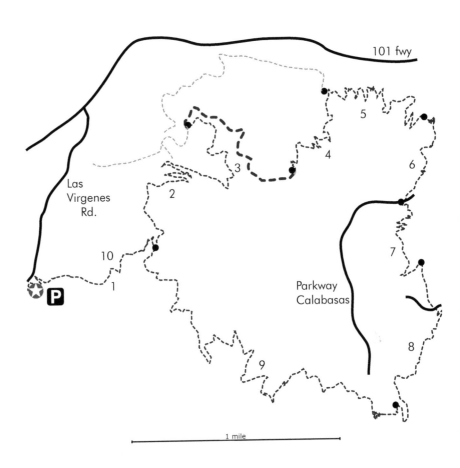

101 fwy

Las
Virgenes
Rd.

Parkway
Calabasas

1 mile

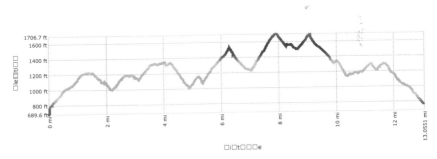

Grassland Trail to Las Virgenes View Trail

Highlights: A beautiful and fun single track trail with lovely views for most of the ride

Miles: 8.6 mile loop

Elevation: 1300 ft

Estimated time: biking: 1.5+hrs

hiking and horseback riding: 3+hrs

Technical: ★★★✦☆

Aerobic: ★★★☆☆

Restrooms: Anza Park, Bark Park

Water: Anza Park, Las Virgenes View Trail

Dogs: on leash

Parking: street parking on Mulholland Hwy is free

Directions to Trailhead: GPS- 34.103556,-118.713611
Mulholland Hwy, Calabasas
101 Fwy: exit 32 for Las Virgenes Rd toward Malibu Canyon. South onto Las Virgenes Rd 3 miles. Right on Mulholland Hwy. Parking along Mulholland Hwy/Las Virgenes Rd.
PCH: north on Malibu Canyon Rd. 4.6 miles, continue on Las Virgenes Rd. 1 mile. Destination is on the left.
*Elevation and mileage are approximate.

Overview: This route can be combined with the Bark Park Tr to Millenium Tr Loop. There is one mile of street riding on Las Virgenes Rd. Some of the trails have signs, others do not. The footing is mostly firm smooth ground that is loose in sections. The hills are moderate with a couple steep hills. The route begins in Malibu Creek State Park off of Mulholland Hwy. The trail is .1 mile west of Las Virgenes Rd on the north side of the street. **(1)** North on Grassland Tr away from the main park entrance paralleling Las Virgenes Rd .3 mile. Grassland Tr has a nice flat to moderate grade. **(2)** Right turn around a power station on asphalt to connect back on the trail. **(3)** The trail bends to the right, crosses a bridge, and comes to a junction .5 mile. **(4)** Follow N. Grassland Tr to the right, cross another bridge 1.5 miles to Anza Park. **(5)** Travel to the right of the park, right at Lost Hills Road, left on Las Virgenes Rd .7 mile to Bark Park. **(6)** Take the Bark Park Tr 1.2 miles to the New Millenium Tr. The trailhead is near the restrooms. The Bark Park Tr is a single track trail with a moderate

Bridge on Grassland Tr

Grassland Trail to Las Virgenes View Trail

grade and a few sharp switchback turns. **(7)** Right turn at Millenium Tr .8 mile. **(8)** Right at intersection on Las Virgenes View Connector Tr. If you are on a bike you will want some momentum to get up the first hill. **(9)** Left turn down a steep, loose, rutted hill. The trail continues 1.4 miles up and down steep hills. **(10)** The trail can be overgrown with tall shrubs

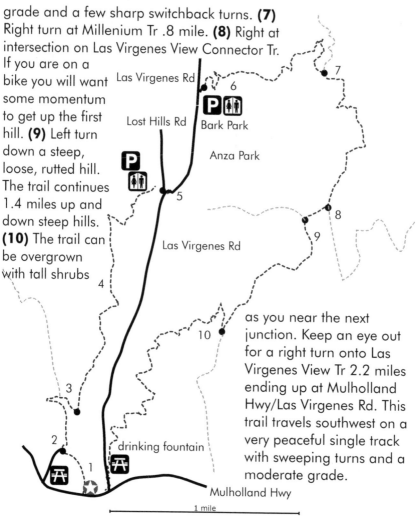

as you near the next junction. Keep an eye out for a right turn onto Las Virgenes View Tr 2.2 miles ending up at Mulholland Hwy/Las Virgenes Rd. This trail travels southwest on a very peaceful single track with sweeping turns and a moderate grade.

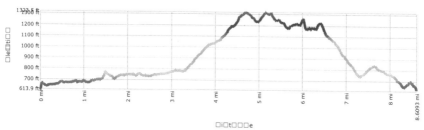

Juan Bautista De Anza to Las Virgenes View Trail

Highlights:	One way trip on a single track with views, ending across from Malibu Creek State Park
Miles:	8 miles one way
Elevation:	1100 ft
Estimated time:	biking: 1-1.5 hrs
	hiking and horseback riding: 2-3 hrs
Technical:	★★★☆☆
Aerobic:	★★★☆☆
Restrooms:	Malibu Creek State Park
Water:	no
Dogs:	on leash
Parking:	parking lot is free at Juan Bautista De Anza; $12 at Malibu Creek State Park, street parking

Directions to Trailhead: GPS - 34.146366,-118.696705
Las Virgenes Rd, Calabasas
101 Fwy: exit 32 Las Virgenes Rd toward Malibu Canyon. Park at the dirt lot next to the Mobil gas station in front of the 101 S off ramp.
Pacific Coast Hwy: north on Malibu Canyon Rd 4.6 miles; continue on Las Virgenes Rd 1.5 mile. Right into the dirt parking lot next to the Mobil gas station.
*Elevation and mileage are approximate.

Anza Loop Tr

Juan Bautista De Anza to Las Virgenes View Trail

Overview: This is an out-and-back or a one-way trip with an opportunity to drop off a car or trailer at one end of the trail with .2 mile on a dirt path alongside Las Virgenes Rd to enter Malibu Creek State Park. Begin the route at Juan Bautista De Anza trailhead next to the Mobil gas station. Travel south ending at Las Virgenes View Tr on the northeast corner of Las Virgenes Rd and Mulholland Hwy. Trailer parking is available at the Juan Bautista De Anza trailhead next to Mobil gas station on the northern end and trailer parking is at the main entrance of Malibu Creek State Park. There is limited street parking on Mulholland Hwy. The trail is a single track heading south. The footing is firm and smooth with some rocks. The grade is moderate with a section of steep short hills. The trail rolls along grassy hills spotted with walnut and oak trees. **(1)** Follow the Juan Bautista De Anza West .3 mile up the hill. **(2)** Right at the junction on the Anza Loop Tr .3 mile. **(3)** Left uphill on the gravel road .2 mile. **(4)** Right on the New Millenium Tr 3.7 miles you will pass the Bark Park Tr on your way to the next unmarked intersection. The trail skirts along the edge of a hillside in full sun leading to a water crossing over a flat rock approximately 5 ft wide. There is a 5-ft drop at the water crossing. The trail follows along the floor through a natural spring and a muddy section that gradually climbs up moderate switcbacks leading to views of Calabasas. The trail follows along the rolling hills leading to a steep section. **(5)** Right at the intersection 1.4 miles as the trail rolls up and down the steep hills with panoramic views. As the brush becomes thicker and you have gone down a few steep hills, keep an eye out on the right for the unmarked Las Virgenes View Tr. **(6)** Right 2.1 miles along the gradual scenic trail with sweeping turns and a section of switchbacks. There is an area where there is a fence alongside a hill with a gradual drop with a blind turn. This trail leads to Las Virgenes Rd/Mulholland Hwy. There is a bench and drinking fountain at the bottom of the trail. This is a good place ot turn around, or to continue to Malibu Creek State Park. Follow Las Virgenes Rd south (left) .2 mile along the dirt path on the side of the road to the main entrance. Bikers and hikers can walk along Mulholland Hwy .1 mile. Left on Grassland Tr leading to Crags Rd. Left on Crags Rd to the parking lot.

Juan Bautista De Anza to Las Virgenes View Trail

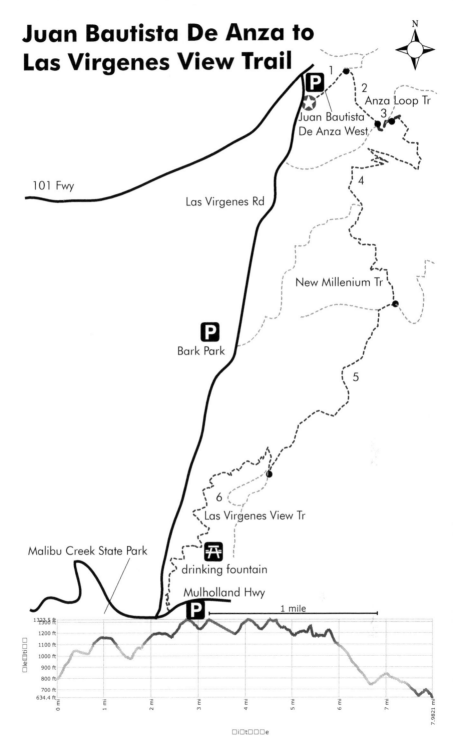

N

1

2

Anza Loop Tr

3

Juan Bautista De Anza West

101 Fwy

Las Virgenes Rd

4

New Millenium Tr

P

Bark Park

5

6

Las Virgenes View Tr

Malibu Creek State Park

drinking fountain

Mulholland Hwy

1 mile

P

1323.5 ft
1300 ft
1200 ft
1100 ft
1000 ft
900 ft
800 ft
700 ft
634.4 ft

0 mi   1 mi   2 mi   3 mi   4 mi   5 mi   6 mi   7 mi   7.9821 mi

Secret Trail/Calabasas 🚴 🛹 🏇 Peak Trail/Red Rock Canyon Park

Highlights:	A one-way trip to Red Rock Canyon Park winding through sandstone peaks on a single track leading to wide fire road and panoramic views
Miles:	4.1 miles one way; 8.2 miles round trip
Elevation:	1800 ft
Estimated time:	biking: 1.5 hrs hiking and horseback riding: 3+hrs
Technical:	★★★⯪☆
Aerobic:	★★★★☆
Restrooms:	Red Rock Cyn Park
Water:	drinking fountain
Dogs:	on leash
Parking:	street parking on Mulholland Hwy for trailers; Street parking on Stunt Rd for automoblies

Directions to Trailhead: GPS 34.12646,-118.657359
Mulholland Hwy, Calabasas
The trailhead is between mile marker 27.34 and 27.53 on Mulholland Hwy between Old Topanga Canyon Rd on the north end and Stunt Rd on the south end and in between both turn offs to Dry Canyon Cold Creek Rd. The dirt area recommended to park autos and trailers is off the street with a wide shoulder on an open stretch on the east side of Mulholland Hwy. Automobiles may also park on Stunt Rd at the Calabasas Peak trailhead.
*Elevation and mileage are approximate.
Overview: Bikes are not allowed on the Secret Tr according to the Topo map; although there aren't any signs. Bikes may begin off of Stunt Rd following the Calabasas Peak Tr up a steep hill, right turn down Red Rock Cyn Tr 1.1 miles leading to the park. This trail begins on a technical single track through the sandstone peaks winding through the canyon through seasonal creek crossings leading to Calabasas Peak Trail. The wide fire road has 360 degree views at the peak climbing up and over the hill leading to Red Rock Canyon Park. Calabasas Peak trail is a steep climb and can have loose footing. There are areas of shade with lush vegetation, beautiful red rock sandstone outcroppings and caves, shaded picnic benches, a restroom and a drinking fountain. **(1)** Begin on the Secret Tr 1.4

Secret Trail/Calabasas Peak Trail/Red Rock Canyon Park

Secret Tr

Red Rock Tr

Secret Trail/Calabasas Peak Trail/Red Rock Canyon Park

miles up the canyon. **(2)** Right turn at the top on Calabasas Peak Tr 1.7 miles. **(3)** At the split there is a bench; left down the Red Rock Tr 1.1 miles leading into Red Rock Canyon Park. To return, go back up Red Rock Tr; right on Calabasas Peak Tr; left on Secret Tr.

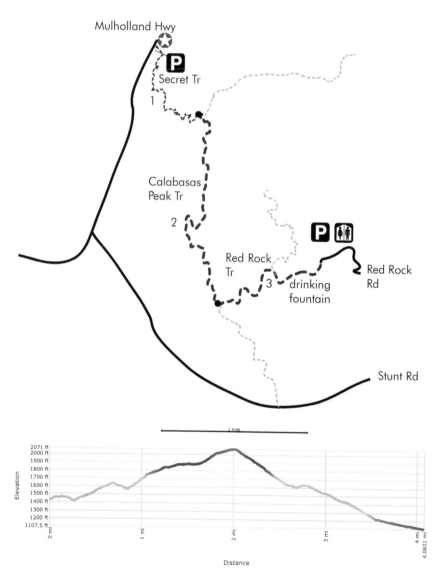

Backbone Trails

Santa Monica Mountains National Recreation Area

The multi-use Backbone Tr runs through the Santa Monica Mountains. They are a must do for mountain biking and hiking with well-maintained, beautiful single track trails running in the east-west direction from Corral Cyn Rd to Yerba Buena Rd. There are approximately 20 miles of multi-use single track trails one-way. The Backbone trails are split up by private property. A popular section of the Backbone Tr for hikers and mountain bikers is from Kanan Rd to Corral Cyn Rd heading east/west on a 6.3 mile stretch of single track. This ride is the most technical and, therefore, best for intermediate to advanced level mountain bikers.

Another beautiful section is travelling west from Kanan Rd for 2.5 miles leading to Zuma Ridge Tr. From this point, approximately .5 mile uphill (south) for an ocean view, or you can connect to another section of the Backbone Tr with street riding on Encinal Cyn Rd west for .7 mile leading to Trancas Cyn in 1.6 miles. This will lead to a parking lot on Encinal Cyn Rd continuing on another portion of the Backbone Tr.

This section is the least technical, very scenic with ocean views. The Backbone Tr climbs for 1.1 miles, crosses Mulholland Hwy and continues for 2.5 miles to Eltz. Meloy Mtwy Fire Rd. The fire road that connects the backbone trail is currently off limits. NOTE: At this time the National Park Service has asked the public to not access the Eltz Meloy Fire Rd due to sensitive negotiations taking place. They are pursuing acquisition of an easement. In the near future we may enjoy the continual trail again.

The Backbone Tr continues 4.4 miles one way heading east with ocean views on a narrow, non-technical trail. This section can be accessed from a parking lot on Yerba Buena Rd across the street from the Mishe Mokwa trailhead.

The Sandstone Peak trailhead south on Yerba Buena Rd is a Backbone Tr for 1.5 miles up a steep rocky trail. This trail is best for hikers, due to the steep rocky trail. Horses can travel up the hill, but only to a point. There is rock scrambling up a huge boulder for .2 mile. The parking lots are small and fill up very quickly on the weekends. Horses should be very comfortable with bikes to use these trails. There are blind turns and drop offs.

Encinal Canyon Road to Yerba Buena Road

Highlights: Picturesque the entire time; mainly single track; ocean views; moderate smooth grade

Miles: 9.2 miles one way, 18.4 round trip

Elevation: 2500 ft

Estimated time: biking: 2+hrs

hiking and horseback riding: 4+hrs

Technical: ★★✫✫✫

Aerobic: ★★★✫✫

Restrooms: no

Water: no

Dogs: on leash

Parking: parking lot is free

Directions to Trailhead: GPS 34.085383,-118.862516
Encinal Canyon Rd, Malibu
101 Fwy: exit 36 for Kanan Rd south 6 miles, Right on
Mulholland Dr 1 mile. At the split follow Encinal Canyon Rd
2 miles. The dirt parking lot is on the right side of the street.
Pacific Coast Hwy: north on Encinal Canyon Rd 5 miles. Turn right to
stay on Encinal Canyon Rd 1 mile. Dirt parking lot is on the left side
of the street.
*Elevation and mileage are approximate.

Overview: NOTE: The trail trespasses through private property on
Eltz Meloy Mtwy. National Park Service has advised the public to not
use Eltz Meloy Mtwy while an easement is being pursued. Check
the NPS website or multiusetrails.com for status. It is a great begin-
ner/intermediate ride. The trail is very pleasant with sweeping turns,
smooth footing, a gradual incline with partial shade and ocean views
on the first 3.5 miles. The fire road that connects the Backbone Tr.
is steep with loose footing. Novice mountain bikers can ride the first
section up to the fire road and then turn around. The last section of
the Backbone Tr is very picturesque with ocean views. The trail is narrow with loose rocks and a moderate grade. There are many blind
turns and at times the trail can have quite a few mountain bikers. The
ride begins from the dirt parking lot on Encinal Cyn Rd. The trailhead
is next to the Clark Ranch Fire Rd. **(1)** Follow the Backbone single
track 1.1 miles on the a moderate grade through the wildflowers

View from Eltz Meloy Fire Rd

Encinal Canyon Road to Yerba Buena Road

and coastal sage scrub. **(2)** Cross Mulholland Hwy and continue on the single track 2.5 miles along the well-maintained trail. **(3)** Left on Etz Meloy Fire Rd 1.4 miles. This is a steep fire road with loose footing at times. It is well worth the climb with ocean views to the south and mountain and lake views to the north. The trail will dead end. **(4)** Go around the fence, down the driveway; left on Yerba Buena Rd 300 ft. **(5)** Backbone Tr continues on the right side of the street. It is hidden, keep an eye out, continue 4.2 miles. The trail is a pleasant, narrow single track with loose rocks and ocean views that gradually climbs up and down the canyon. The trail will end up at a parking lot on Yerba Buena Rd across the street from Mishe Mokwa trailhead.

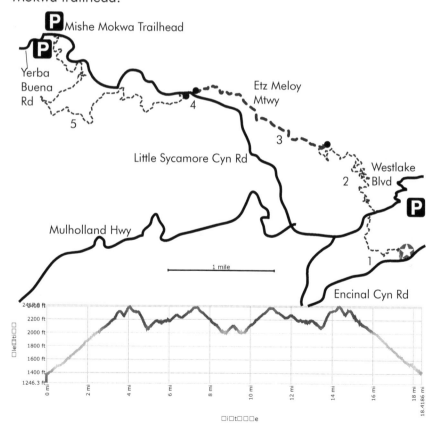

Sandstone Peak Trail

Highlights:	Steep trail to the highest point in the Santa Monica Mountains with amazing 360 views
Miles:	1.5 miles one way
Elevation:	1000 ft
Estimated time:	biking: 45 mins: 1 hr hiking and horseback riding: 1+hrs
Technical:	★★★★☆
Aerobic:	★★★★☆
Restrooms:	yes
Water:	no
Dogs:	on leash
Parking:	Yerba Buena parking lot is free

Directions to Trailhead: GPS 34.111467,-118.926723
Sandstone Peak Trailhead, Yerba Buena Rd, Malibu
101 Fwy: exit 36 for Westlake Blvd. South on Westlake Blvd 5.1 miles. Left on Mulholland Hwy 2.1 miles. Right on Little Sycamore Canyon Rd 1.9 miles. Continue on Yerba Buena Rd. 2.7 miles. Destination is on the right.
Pacific Coast Hwy: Turn right on Yerba Buena 3.2 miles. Turn right to stay on Yerba Buena Rd 1.2 miles. Take first left to stay on Yerba Buena Rd. Turn right to stay on Yerba Buena Rd. 1.5 miles. Destination is on the left.
*Elevation and mileage are approximate.
Overview: This out-and-back route is steep and rocky, so walking sticks are recommended. There is rock scrambling up the last .2 mile. This route begins at the Yerba Buena/Sandstone Peak parking lot. The parking lot is on the west side of the street. Coming from the 101 Freeway, the trailhead is on the right. You will pass 2 small dirt parking lots just across the street from each other. It is approximately .5 mile from there. The sign for the parking lot is sometimes hidden by the brush. The parking lot is small, but large enough to fit horse trailers. The entrance to the parking lot is rocky. **(1)** Begin up the trail heading north 1.3 miles. You will pass a junction for the Mishe Mokwa Tr. The Mishe Mokwa Tr. is hiking only. The trail makes a nice loop connecting to sandstone peak. At the Mishe Mokwa Tr junction, stay to the left and continue up the steep rocky hill. Walking sticks are recommended for this hike because it is steep and can be slick rom the loose rocks. **(2)** There will be a sign at the next junction. Turn

Top of Sandstone Peak

Sandstone Peak Trail

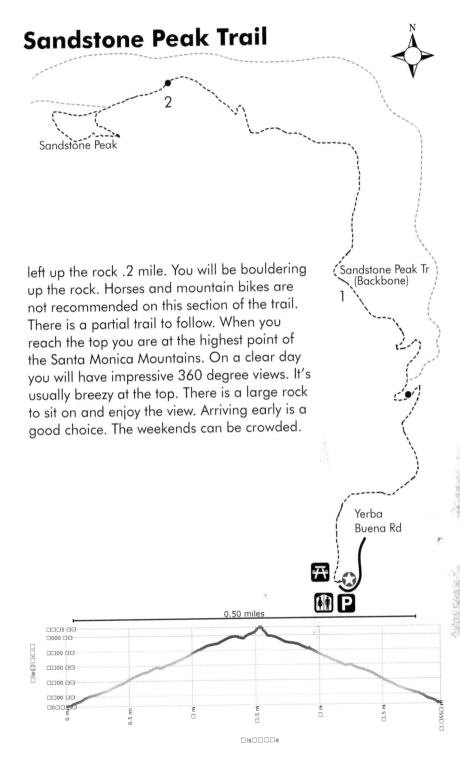

2

Sandstone Peak

Sandstone Peak Tr
(Backbone)

1

left up the rock .2 mile. You will be bouldering up the rock. Horses and mountain bikes are not recommended on this section of the trail. There is a partial trail to follow. When you reach the top you are at the highest point of the Santa Monica Mountains. On a clear day you will have impressive 360 degree views. It's usually breezy at the top. There is a large rock to sit on and enjoy the view. Arriving early is a good choice. The weekends can be crowded.

Yerba
Buena Rd

0.50 miles

Kanan Road to Corral Canyon Road

Highlights:	98% single track; obstacles; seasonal creek crossings; scenic; partial shade
Miles:	6.3 miles one way; 12.6 miles round trip
Elevation:	2600 ft
Estimated time:	biking: 3 hrs
	hiking and horseback riding: 6 hrs
Technical:	★★★★☆
Aerobic:	★★★★☆
Restrooms:	yes
Water:	no
Dogs:	on leash
Parking:	parking lot is free

Directions to Trailhead: GPS 34.07607,-118.815449
Backbone Trailhead, Kanan Rd, Malibu
101 Fwy: exit 36 for Kanan Rd. South, approximately 7.5 miles. Destination will be on the right side.
Pacific Coast Hwy: north on Kanan Dume Rd approximately 4 miles. Destination will be on the left side.
*Elevation and mileage are approximate.

Overview: Popular mountain bike trail with many blind turns. The footing changes frequently from firm, smooth ground to loose rocks and sandstone. The hills range from moderate to steep sections. This is an intermediate to advanced bike ride. The single track begins at Kanan Rd travels east and ends at Corral Canyon Rd parking lot.

Riding up from Corral Cyn

Kanan Road/Corral Canyon Road

(1) The toughest section is the beginning of the trail climbing approximately .1 mile up and over the tunnel. The hill is very steep and rocky. At the top of the hill, the hills become moderate, but the trail rarely levels off, always descending or ascending with a couple steep hills. After .3 mile the trail crosses Newton Cyn and continues winding in and out of the canyon with some tight switchbacks and trees to maneuver around. There is some shade including sections of poison oak alongside the trail. **(2)** Follow the trail 1.9 miles to Latigo Cyn Rd. **(3)** Cross Latigo Cyn Rd. The trail descends down the hill, over railroad ties, and back up a long steep hill that some mountain bikers push their bikes up. **(4)** After 1.5 miles, right on a fire road for 100 ft. Left down the trail leading to Corral Cyn. This is the most technical section of the trail with many creek crossings and rocks to maneuver around. The trail intersects a fire road. **(5)** Left on the fire road .1 mile. **(6)** Left on the Backbone Tr .3 mile to Corral Cyn parking lot. Return the way you came.

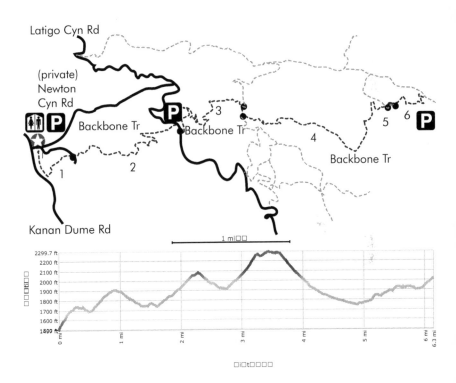

Backbone Trail/
Trancas Canyon

Highlights:	Scenic single track climbs in and out of the canyons with partial shade
Miles:	5.3 miles one way; 10.6 miles round trip
Elevation:	2200 ft
Estimated time:	biking: 1.5-2.5 hrs
	hiking and horseback riding: 3-4 hrs
Technical:	★★★☆☆
Aerobic:	★★★½☆
Restrooms:	yes
Water:	no
Dogs:	on leash
Parking:	parking lot on Kanan Rd is free

Directions to Trailhead: GPS 34.07607,-118.815449
Backbone Trailhead, Kanan Rd, Malibu
101 Fwy: exit 36 for Kanan Rd. South approximately 7.5 miles. Destination will be on the right side.
Pacific Coast Hwy: north on Kanan Dume Rd approximately 4 miles. Destination will be on the left side.
*Elevation and mileage are approximate.

Overview: This route is an out-and-back. The elevation includes round trip. This is a picturesque, non-technical, single track with a lot of climbing. This is a good trail for a windy day. The trail is lined with tall shrubs and trees most of the time. The footing is firm with rocky sections. The climbs are moderate. There is .75 mile of street travel each way. This route begins at the Kanan parking lot at the Backbone trailhead approximately one mile south of Mulholland Hwy. There is additional parking .1 mile north of the parking lot on Kanan Rd in a dirt lot. There is a trail from the dirt lot that connects to the Backbone Tr without having to travel along Kanan Rd. Hikers and equestrians may prefer to turn around at Zuma Ridge Tr. **(1)** From the trailhead head west away from Kanan Rd. The trail drops in and out of the canyons, crosses a couple bridges, and travels along canopies of trees in the canyons with lush vegetation. After approximately 2 miles, you'll pass a cut off for Zuma Falls, a seasonal waterfall that you can see from a distance on the right side of the trail. There is not a sign and the trail can become overgrown. Continue .5 mile to

Backbone Tr

Backbone Trail/Trancas Canyon

Zuma Ridge Tr **(2)** When the trail comes to a T turn right on Zuma Ridge Tr .3 mile. **(3)** Left on Encinal Cyn Rd .7 mile. **(4)** At mile marker 1.32 on Encinal Cyn Rd there is a trail on the (left) south side of the street. It is well hidden. Follow the Trancas Edison Rd .3 mile up a moderate hill to a junction. **(5)** The trail to the left leads to private property. Slight right following the Backbone Tr 1.6 miles to Encinal Cyn Rd. Turn around and return the same way. If you want a longer ride, cross Encinal Cyn Rd to connect directly to more Backbone trails.

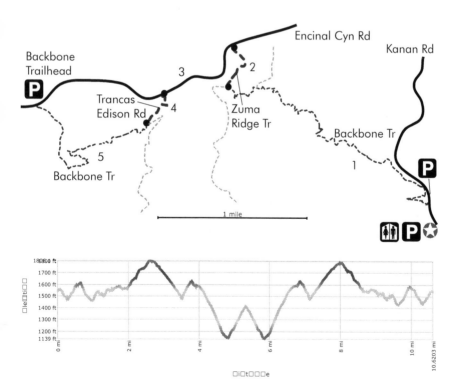

Charmlee Wilderness Park

City of Malibu Parks and Recreation Department

Charmlee Wilderness Park consists of 550 acres of coastal terrain, oak groves, coastal sage scrub, and chaparral. Charmlee offers picnic areas, a porta potty, a nature center, and a drinking fountain. The Nature Center is open Saturday and Sunday 8-5. Public hikes, school and group nature programs, and interpretive programs are available. This area is not a popular destination; it is common to see only one other person. There are 8 miles of multi-use trails inside of the park with trails leading outside of the park. It is difficult to get lost among the network of trails. This area seems best for a short pleasant hike, bike, and horseback ride. Parking is $4. Park hours are 8 am-sunset 7 days per week. There are two sections of dirt along side Encinal Cyn Rd large enough to park a horse trailer just outside the entrance gates.

Charmlee Park

Charmlee Wilderness

Highlights: Peaceful getaway with ocean and mountain views; stroll through the oak groves and meadows with miles of coastline views

Miles: 3.1 miles

Elevation: 550 ft

Estimated time: mountain biking: 45 mins

hiking and horseback riding: 1 hr

Technical: ★★★✦☆

Aerobic: ★★✦☆☆

Restrooms: porta potty

Water: drinking fountain

Dogs: on leash

Parking: Charlee parking lot is $4

Directions to Trailhead: GPS 34.061166,-118.876952
2577 Encinal Cyn Rd, Malibu 310-457-7247
101 Fwy: exit 36 for Kanan Rd. South on Kanan Rd 6.1 miles. Right on Mulholland Hwy .9 mile. Left on Encinal Cyn Rd 3.5 miles. Turn left to stay on Encinal Cyn Rd 1.2 miles. Destination is on the right. Pacific Coast Hwy: turn on Encinal Cyn Rd north 3.8 miles. Destination is on the left.
*Elevation and mileage are approximate.

Overview: This route is scenic the entire time. The area has many short trails all connecting to each other. This is a counterclockwise loop with a few short, steep hills. The trail wanders through the oak grove along a meadow and enters upon an overlook with ocean views for miles. **(1)** Beginning at the informational kiosk heading go west (right) up the asphalt road past the nature center. **(2)** Left at junction on Potrero Rd. Up the wide gravel road and pass the turn off to the tank. Continue down the steep rutted hill. **(3)** Left on Matt Kouba Tr through the oak grove. **(4)** Right on Clyde Cyn Tr through the grassy field with coastline views. **(5)** Right to stay on Clyde Cyn Tr up a steep hill. **(6)** Right on Clyde Cyn Tr towards the ocean. **(7)** Right on the Reservoir Tr .2 mile to the old reservoir with beautiful views. Follow the cement. The trail continues on the right side heading down a hill. **(8)** Right at the bottom of the hill on the Lower Loop Ocean Overlook Tr (park boundary) overlooking miles of coastline. **(9)** For a beautiful view spot, take the right leading down the trail. Back up the hill, right up the steep, rocky hill. **(10)** Right on E

Charmlee Wilderness

Meadow Tr. **(11)** Stay straight to continue on Botany Tr. There are benches under a shady area with a drinking fountain and a water spicket. Continue straight back to the parking area.

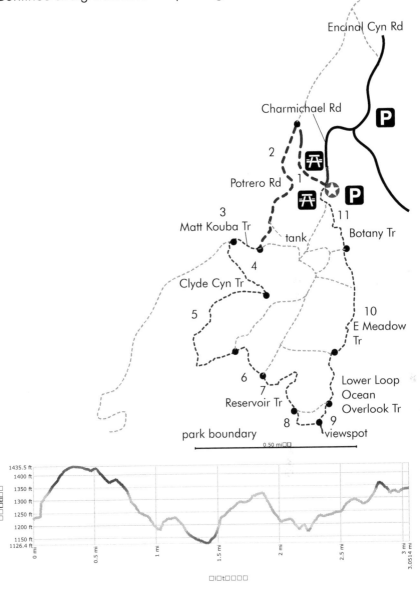

Zuma / Trancas Canyon

The Santa Monica Mountains National Recreation Area

A peaceful wilderness area with approximately 18 miles of trails located north of PCH on Bonsall Dr in Malibu. The south entrance has two trailheads, Bonsall Drive and Busch Drive. The north entrance is located on Kanan Rd at the Backbone trail heading west. The Backbone Trail leads to the Zuma Ridge Trail which runs north and south continuing for 6 miles to Busch Drive. Most of Zuma Ridge Trail is in full sun and dries well after a rain. The only single track that bikes are allowed on is the Backbone Trail off of Kanan Rd. The other single tracks just off of Busch Drive and Bonsall Drive are hiking and horseback riding only. There is a large dirt parking lot at the north end of Bonsall Drive. There is ample room for horse trailers, although the parking lot does get full on the weekends. Porta potties, a hitching post, picnic tables, a hose and bucket, and trash cans are available at the south end of the parking lot. Busch Dr also offers parking on a small dirt lot without amenities.

Top of Zuma Edison Rd

Backbone Trail/Kanan Rd 🚴 🚶 🐎

Highlights: The Backbone Tr crosses over bridges, passes a waterfall, connects to Zuma Ridge Tr, drops down a canyon with ocean views, and a long climb with 1.2 miles street riding on Kanan Rd.

Miles: 11.7

Elevation: 2700 ft

Estimated time: biking: 2+hrs
hiking and horseback riding: 4+hrs

Technical: ★★★☆☆

Aerobic: ★★★★☆

Restrooms: no

Water: no

Dogs: on leash

Parking: parking lot is free

Directions to Trailhead: GPS 34.07607,-118.815449
Backbone Trailhead, Kanan Rd, Malibu
101 Fwy: exit 36 for Kanan Rd. South approximately 7.5 miles. Destination will be on the right side.
Pacific Coast Hwy: north on Kanan Dume Rd approximately 4 miles. Destination will be on the left side.
*Elevation and mileage are approximate.

Overview: Backbone Trail is a popular hiking and mountain biking trail. After passing Backbone Tr, the area becomes very remote. This route is great for anyone who loves climbing a non-technical trail in solitude. There are 1.2 miles of street riding on Kanan Rd. **(1)** The single track begins at Kanan Rd opposite of the tunnel. Travel west on the Backbone Tr in and out of the canyons, cross a couple bridges under canopies of trees and lush foliage along with exposed areas of full sun 2.5 miles. **(2)** The trail intersects with Zuma Ridge Tr. South (left turn) 3.2 miles. Zuma Ridge Tr extends from Encinal Cyn Rd to Busch Dr near PCH with wonderful ocean views. **(3)** The trail connects with Zuma Edison Fire Rd. Left on th fire road, go around the gate 4.1 miles east winding in and out of the canyons. There is a horse waterer .5 mile down Zuma Edison Rd. "Not for Human Consumption" is posted on the water tank. This trail descends 1.9 miles quickly becoming more lush as the trail approaches the creek. This is a good place to rest in the shade before the steep hill 2.2 miles. At the top of the hill, the trail levels off. You will pass Zuma Cyn

Zuma Cyn Connector Trail

Backbone Trail/Kanan Rd

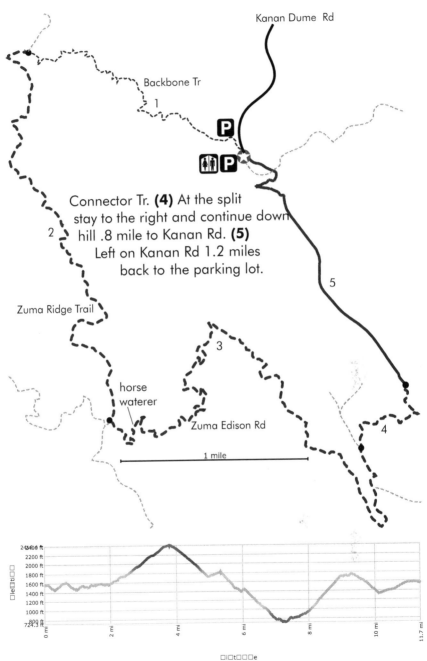

Kanan Dume Rd

Backbone Tr

1

Connector Tr. **(4)** At the split
stay to the right and continue down
2 hill .8 mile to Kanan Rd. **(5)**
Left on Kanan Rd 1.2 miles
back to the parking lot.

5

Zuma Ridge Trail

3

horse
waterer

Zuma Edison Rd

4

1 mile

Zuma Loop

Highlights:	Single track trail with lush vegetation through the canyons with ocean and canyon views
Miles:	4.2 miles
Elevation:	1000 ft
Estimated time:	hiking and horseback riding: 1-1.5 hrs
Technical:	★★✦☆☆
Aerobic:	★★★☆☆
Restrooms:	porta potty
Water:	hose
Dogs:	on leash
Parking:	dirt parking lot is free

Directions to Trailhead: GPS 34.031544,-118.812042
Bonsall Dr. Malibu
101 Fwy: exit 36 for Kanan Rd south 12 miles. Right on Pacific Coast Hwy 1 mile. Before Zuma Beach turn right on Bonsall 1 mile. Destination will be at the end of the street.
Pacific Coast Hwy: north on Bonsall 1 mile. Destination will be at the end of the street.
*Elevation and mileage are approximate.

Overview: This is a beautiful hiking and equestrian trail. Bikes are not allowed on single track trails in Zuma/Trancas Canyon or in lower Zuma Canyon. The trail system is well marked.

Canyon View Trail

Zuma Loop

Restrooms, picnic benches, and a hose are at the south end of the parking lot. The grade is moderate, and the footing is firm with few rocks and is partially rutted. **(1)** Head north away from the restrooms at the Bonsall parking lot .2 mile on Zuma Cyn Tr. **(2)** Left on the Zuma Loop Tr 1.1 miles through the wash with walnut, sycamore, willow, and oak trees. **(3)** Left on Scenic Tr .2 mile. The trail has lush vegetation along the east side of the loop. **(4)** Left on Cyn View Tr 1.4 miles as the trail climbs up the ridge and along the canyon walls. **(5)** Right on Ocean View Tr descending down the hill with beautiful ocean views among coastal sage scrub. **(6)** Left on Zuma Cyn Tr .2 mile to return along the base of the canyon.

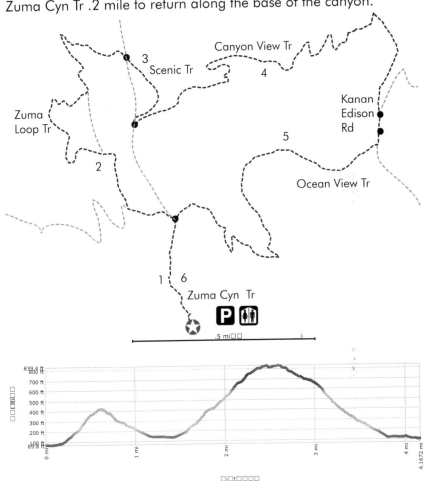

Big Zuma Loop

Highlights:	Strenuous but scenic trail with lush vegetation; up the canyons with ocean and canyon views
Miles:	10.7 miles
Elevation:	2600 ft
Estimated time:	hiking and horseback riding: 4+hrs
Technical:	★★✦☆☆
Aerobic:	★★★★☆
Restrooms:	no
Water:	no
Dogs:	on leash
Parking:	dirt parking lot is free

Directions to Trailhead: GPS 34.033717,-118.817953
Busch Dr, Malibu
101 Fwy: exit 36 for Kanan Rd south 12 miles. Right on PCH 1 mile. Right on Busch Dr .8 mile. Turn right to continue on Busch Dr approximately 1 mile. Destination is at the end of the street.
PCH: north on Busch Dr 8 miles Right and continue on Busch Dr approximately 1 mile. Destination is at the end of the street.
*Elevation and mileage are approximate.

Overview: Bikes are allowed on the fire roads only in Zuma Trancas Cyn. This loop is very scenic and very strenuous. The footing is hard packed with rocks and ruts in places. The grade is moderate with a long steep climb. Bring water with you. There isn't water available for humans. There is an automatic horse water after the first climb and a seasonal creek at the bottom of Zuma Edison Fire Rd just before the big climb up the hill. There is a hose at the Bonsall parking lot with porta potties .2 mile south of Zuma Cyn Tr at mile 10. The trail system is well marked. The trails can also be accessed from Bonsall trailhead. **(1)** Beginning on Busch Dr north on Zuma Ridge Tr 2.7 miles climbing steadily with 1200 ft elevation gain. The trail skirts along the edge of the mountain with ocean and mountain views. **(2)** Soon after passing Trancas Edison Rd, turn right going around the gate on Zuma Edison Fire Rd 4.1 miles. There is an automatic horse waterer approximately .5 mile down the hill. This trail descends 1.9 miles quickly becoming more lush as the trail approaches the creek. There is some shade and rocks to rest on before the big climb up the mountain with full sun gaining 1200 ft. in 2.1 miles. **(3)** Once the trail reaches the top, right turn on Zuma Canyon Connector Trail

Big Zuma Loop

.8 mile gradually descending down the single track leading to Kanan Edison Rd. **(4)** Turn right on Kanan Edison Rd 1.4 miles along the moderate trail with ocean views. **(5)** Soon after passing Canyon View Tr turn right on Ocean View Tr 1.1 miles. This trail is a single track rutted out by horses and gradually descending down to the base of the canyon. **(6)** Cross Zuma Canyon Tr to Ridge Access Tr .7 mile with switchbacks up to Busch Dr *an extra .2 miles on Zuma Cyn Tr through the Bonsall parking lot to the restrooms and horse waterer if needed.

Zuma Ridge Tr

Big Zuma Loop

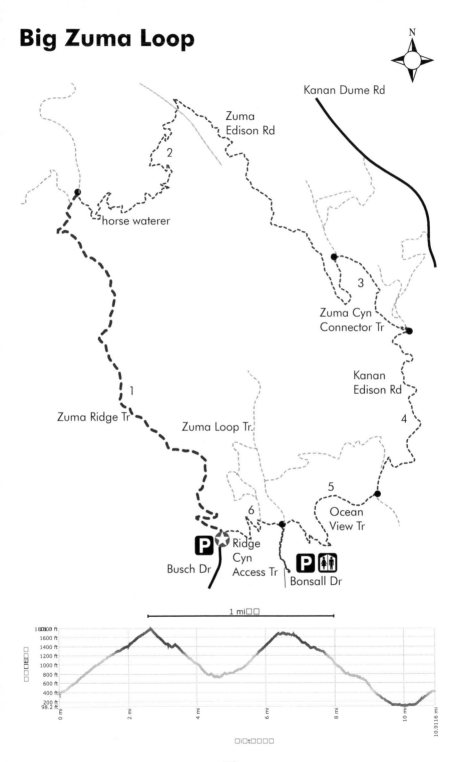

Happy Camp Canyon Regional Park

Santa Monica Mountains Conservancy County of Ventura
E. Ventura County Conservation Authority

A 3,000-acre park with 12.5 miles of trails located at the eastern portion of Moorpark. Happy Camp Canyon Regional Park enjoyed by hikers, equestrians, and occasional mountain bikers. The Happy Camp Canyon trail is the main trail on the valley floor traveling throughout the canyon with an abundance of oak forests, grasslands, and wildflowers. The trail runs from one end of the park to the other with connecting trails. The Middle Range Fire Road skirts along the ridgeline with stunning views running from one end of the park to the other. The two trails connect making a large loop. In the canyons the footing is mostly sand, hard packed in some areas, and very soft in others. The single track that connects Happy Camp Canyon Fire Road to the Middle Range Fire Road is approximately one mile, steep, rutted, and the footing can be loose in areas. The Middle Range Fire Road that runs along the ridge of the mountain is rocky with sections of hard packed dirt and very loose sand. This area is very peaceful and secluded. From the equestrian parking lot, the trail begins above a golf course ascending down a moderate hill for one mile leading to an intersection. There is an informational kiosk with a map of the area and detailed descriptions of the plants and animals that may be seen in the area. Dogs are not allowed past the informational kiosk. Happy Camp does not get crowded on weekends or holidays. There are two main parking areas, an equestrian upper dirt parking lot located on 14105 Broadway equipped with a porta potty. The lower dirt parking lot for cars is .5 mile on Happy Camp Canyon from the Campus Drive intersection. Hours are dawn to dusk.

Happy Camp Cyn Tr

Happy Camp Loop

Highlights:	A walk through the oak tree forest on a sandy bottom; climb along the ridge leading to panoramic views
Miles:	10.9 miles
Elevation:	1400 ft
Estimated time:	biking: 1.5-2 hrs
	hiking and horseback riding: 4-5 hrs
Technical:	★★ ☆ ☆ ☆
Aerobic:	★★★ ☆ ☆
Restrooms:	porta potty at equestrian trailhead
Water:	no
Dogs:	dogs are not allowed past the kiosk
Parking:	Lower parking lot, Equestrian parking lot, sometimes a $4 fee, and sometimes free. Be sure to check at the entrance.

Directions to Trailhead: GPS 34.315359,-118.87428
Equestrian Parking Lot,14105 Broadway, Moorpark
23 Fwy: exit Los Angeles Ave west on Los Angeles Ave 1.2 miles. Right (north) on Moorpark Rd .6 mile. Moorpark turns into Walnut Canyon 2.1 miles. The street will take a left turn. Stay straight for 200 ft. Right on Broadway .2 miles to the end of the road
Lower Parking Lot,15100 Happy Camp Canyon Road, Moorpark
118 Fwy: exit Princeton Ave north to Campus Drive. Left on Campus Drive for .5 mile to Happy Camp Canyon Regional Park. Parking is to the right of the golf course.
*Elevation and mileage are approximate.

Overview: There isn't any water available on this ride and little shade once you reach Big Mountain. This trail makes a great horseback ride and hike, but the deep sand can be difficult for a bike. The footing has many sandy sections with firm ground on the top of the mountain with loose rocks, rutted at times. The grade is moderate with a steep, rutted hill. The trail begins at the equestrian parking lot off of Broadway. The trail may begin for hikers and mountain bikers at the trailhead off of Happy Camp Cyn Rd next to the golf course walking around the golf course to the junction. **(1)** Follow Happy Camp Rd to the kiosk. Overlooking the golf course and the surrounding mountains, the trail ascends down the gradual hill 1.1 miles. **(2)** When the trail levels off on Happy Camp Cyn

Happy Camp Cyn Tr

Happy Camp Loop

Fire Rd, travel .4 mile to the informational kiosk. **(3)** The trail comes to a junction, stay along the flat trail slight left. Continue along the canyon floor through the sand 3 miles. There is a feeling of isolation as the trail gets deeper into the oak forest without a single house in sight. **(4)** As the trail nears the end of the park, there is a split in the trail, stay to the right .6 miles to the shady rest area with a picnic bench and two hitching posts. **(5)** The trail turns into a single track 1 mile up a steep hill reaching the top of Big Mountain. This section of the trail is rutted and steep. Once you have reached the top of the hill, you are surrounded by panoramic views. The fire road is firm with rocks in places.

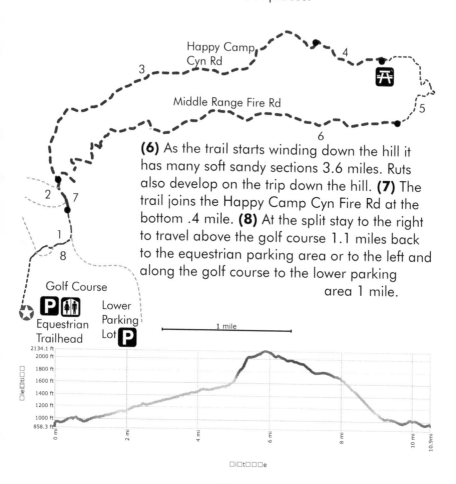

(6) As the trail starts winding down the hill it has many soft sandy sections 3.6 miles. Ruts also develop on the trip down the hill. **(7)** The trail joins the Happy Camp Cyn Fire Rd at the bottom .4 mile. **(8)** At the split stay to the right to travel above the golf course 1.1 miles back to the equestrian parking area or to the left and along the golf course to the lower parking area 1 mile.

Arroyo Conejo Open Space

Conejo Open Space Conservation Agency

The Arroyo Conejo Open Space includes 302 acres in the Conejo Valley located north of the northeast corner of Hillcrest and Ventu Park a.k.a. the Barranca. With a perennial stream, deep canyon walls, and riparian woodlands along the valley floor, this area is wonderful to visit anytime especially during the summer. This is the main point of entry down the canyon with connecting trails leading to Conejo Cyns and Wildwood. The trail leading to Conejo Canyons is wide, flat, shaded by oak woodlands with grassy meadows. There are two trails leading to Wildwood. The trail leading directly to Wildwood is a technical steep trail, climbing above the Lynnmere neighborhood connecting with the Lynnmere Tr. with little shade surrounded by coastal sage scrub. The trail leading to Wildwood takes you through Conejo Canyons along the Arroyo Conejo Creek, and across Hill Canyon Rd. This area has become more popular with the recent bridge installed just off of Hill Canyon Rd. There are restrooms and drinking fountains inside the park. The parking lot is large enough to park horse trailers, although the parking lot fills up quickly during little league games on the weekends and after school. An option is to park on Calle Yucca or Rancho Conejo.

Arroyo Conejo Tr

Arroyo Conejo Trail

Highlights: Many creek crossings; peaceful; great for a hot day with some shade along the wide trail

Miles: 4 miles one way; 8 miles round trip

Elevation: 1000 ft round trip

Estimated time: biking: 1-1.5 hrs
hiking and horseback riding: 2-2.5 hrs

Technical: ★★ ☆ ☆ ☆

Aerobic: ★★ ☆ ☆ ☆

Restrooms: Rancho Conejo Playfields Park

Water: drinking fountain

Dogs: on leash

Parking: Rancho Conejo Playfields parking lot is free

Directions to Trailhead: GPS 34.191065,-118.91137
Rancho Conejo Playfields 950 N Ventu Park, Newbury Park
101 Fwy: exit Ventu Park. North on Ventu Park .3 mile to Rancho Conejo Playfields on the right side of the street.
*Elevation and mileage are approximate.

Overview: Elevation shows one way. The trail follows Arroyo Conejo Creek. Expect to get your feet wet. **(1)** Head northwest alongside the park on a ridge with views of the deep rustic canyons and the houses above the canyon 1.3 miles. The trail begins as a single track for one mile. At the split stay slight right. The trail widens as you descend down into the canyon. There is a pretty little waterfall on the left side of the trail as you come close to the first water crossing. At the bottom of the hill there aren't any houses in sight, and its very peaceful. **(2)** Left after the creek on the flat, wide trail 1.2 miles. The trail is filled with riparian woodlands and traverses the creek many times with bridges and rocks at some of the crossings. The bridges have been recently placed, but they can wash away after a heavy rain. This trail leads to Conejo Canyons in Santa Rosa Valley. Some of the rocks in the water for crossing are unstable. **(3)** After passing the water treatment plant is an uphill. There is a single track on the right side of the hill about 30 ft up the hill. Follow the single track .3 mile to a junction. **(4)** Straight through the intersection 1.1 miles. Horses can continue on the trail instead of going over the bridge. Go through the last deep water which leads to the parking lot. Follow the same route for the return trip. Hikers and bikers can make a right after .9 mile. Cross the bridge to Hill

Arroyo Conejo Tr.

Arroyo Conejo Trail

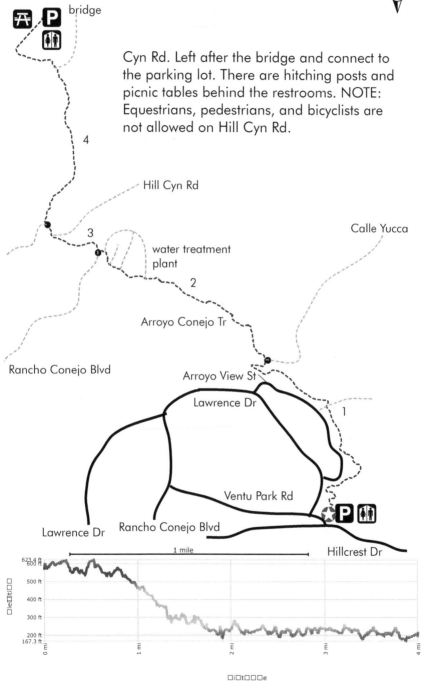

Cyn Rd. Left after the bridge and connect to the parking lot. There are hitching posts and picnic tables behind the restrooms. NOTE: Equestrians, pedestrians, and bicyclists are not allowed on Hill Cyn Rd.

bridge

4

Hill Cyn Rd

3

water treatment plant

2

Calle Yucca

Arroyo Conejo Tr

Rancho Conejo Blvd

Arroyo View St

Lawrence Dr

1

Ventu Park Rd

Lawrence Dr   Rancho Conejo Blvd

Hillcrest Dr

Arroyo Conejo to Wildwood

Highlights:	Single track; waterfall; views, many water crossings; shady picnic area; rocky sections
Miles:	4.6 miles one way; 9.2 miles out and back
Elevation:	2100 ft out and back
Estimated time:	biking: 2 hrs hiking & horseback riding: 3.5- 4 hrs
Technical:	★★★✦☆
Aerobic:	★★★★☆
Restrooms:	Rancho Conejo Playfields, rest area in Wildwood
Water:	wood
Dogs:	on leash
Parking:	parking lot is free

Directions to Trailhead: GPS 34.191065,-118.91137
Rancho Conejo Playfields 950 N Ventu Park, Newbury Park
101 Fwy: exit Ventu Park. North on Ventu Park .3 mile to Rancho Conejo Playfields on the right side of the street.
*Elevation and mileage are approximate.

Overview: This out-and-back route connects to Wildwood Park. This route has a lot of climbing. It is recommended for horseback riding, hiking, and mountain biking. There is a steep technical section on Lynnmere Tr. Beginning at the Rancho Conejo Playfields on Ventu Park. The trailhead is at the east end of the parking lot. There isn't much shade for most of the ride until the rest area. **(1)** Cross the stepover and follow the single track along the fence 1 mile. **(2)** Slight right when the trail splits. Go around the gate and down the hill .3 mile. **(3)** Cross the creek and turn right on the trail for approximately 300 ft then turn left and the trail ascends up a steep hill north .4 mile alongside houses. **(4)** At the Lynnmere Tr junction stay to the right. Cross the tall stepovers at Calle Yucca St. There are steep, rocky, technical sections on this trail. This trail is lined with chaparral and coastal sage scrub. The trail runs along some houses and above a neighborhood .8 mile. **(5)** At the junction, stay to the left .4 mile. After crossing Lynnmere Dr, continue on the other side. **(6)** At the T junction turn left and follow the Lynnmere Tr .7 mile on the popular mountain biking and hiking trail. **(7)** At the next junction, cross a small wooden bridge and turn right descending down the

Arroyo Conejo Tr

Arroyo Conejo to Wildwood

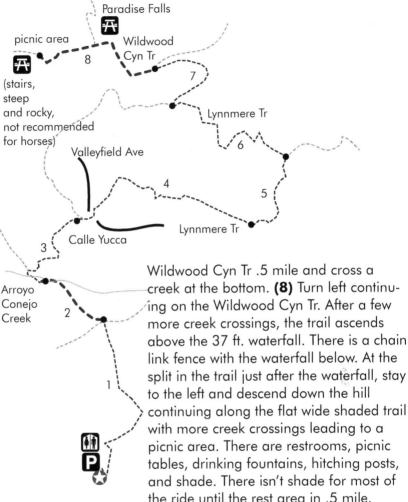

Paradise Falls

picnic area

Wildwood
Cyn Tr

8

7

(stairs,
steep
and rocky,
not recommended
for horses)

Lynnmere Tr

Valleyfield Ave

6

4

5

Calle Yucca

Lynnmere Tr

3

Arroyo
Conejo
Creek

2

1

Wildwood Cyn Tr .5 mile and cross a creek at the bottom. **(8)** Turn left continuing on the Wildwood Cyn Tr. After a few more creek crossings, the trail ascends above the 37 ft. waterfall. There is a chain link fence with the waterfall below. At the split in the trail just after the waterfall, stay to the left and descend down the hill continuing along the flat wide shaded trail with more creek crossings leading to a picnic area. There are restrooms, picnic tables, drinking fountains, hitching posts, and shade. There isn't shade for most of the ride until the rest area in .5 mile.

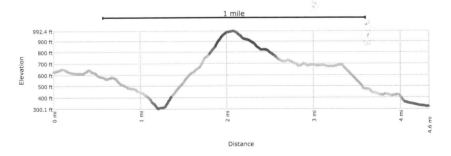

Potrero Ridge/Dos Vientos

Conejo Open Space Conservation Agency

Dos Vientos/Portrero Ridge encompasses approximately 1,400 acres of open space located at the southwest section of the Conejo Valley at the edge of the Camarillo grade running east/west from Wendy Drive. The area is adjacent to the Rancho Sierra Vista/Satwiwa National Park/Point Mugu State Park. The weather is a bit cooler than other surrounding areas being closer to the ocean which is a great option for a hot day. The area also dries well after a rain. The grassy hillsides, oak woodlands, coastal sage scrub, and chaparral can be accessed from over a dozen trailheads with street parking and a few parking lots. The parking lots to access trailheads are at the south end of Wendy Dr or Potrero Rd west of Wendy Dr for the Potrero Ridge Trail capacity to hold approximately 10 cars, Reino Rd north of Lynn Rd for the Potrero Ridge Trail (gates open at sunrise and close at 4 pm.) The gravel lot is large and behind gates. The parking lot is closed after rains until the trails are dry. Dos Vientos Community Park to access Conejo Mountain trail and Twin Ponds is not behind gates. The parking lots are large enough for automobiles and horse trailers.

The trails are multi-use and well-maintained with a moderate grade. The majority of the trails connect throughout the community in the hillsides above neighborhoods with views of the surrounding mountains and the coastline. Many of the trails are short in length, but can be linked together with street crossing within a stones throw of houses. It is easy to get lost; it is recommended to bring a map with you. Some of the crosswalks have raised buttons suitable for equestrians mounted on horseback. The trails that run along the neighborhood streets have stepovers with decomposed granite sidewalks bounded by a fence rail. This is a great area for hiking, horseback riding, and mountain biking.

Potrero Ridge to Twin Ponds

Highlights: Single track climbs along the hilltops leading to Twin Ponds; views

Miles: 9.7 miles

Elevation: 1750 ft

Estimated time: biking: 1.5 -2 hrs
hiking and horseback riding: 3.5-4 hrs

Technical: ★★★☆☆

Aerobic: ★★★☆☆

Restrooms: Dos Vientos Community Park

Water: Dos Vientos Community Park

Dogs: on leash

Parking: parking lot is free - open sunrise to 4.

Directions to Trailhead: GPS 34.165436,-118.95781
Portrero Ridge Trailhead, Reino Rd, Newbury Park
101 Fwy north: exit Borchard Rd south onto Borchard Rd/Rancho Conejo Blvd 2 miles. Left on Reino Rd 1 mile. Turn right into the driveway on the right past Dunaway Dr.
101 Fwy south: exit Wendy Dr. South on Wendy Dr 1 mile. Right on Borchard Rd .5 mile. Left on S. Reino Rd 1 mile. Turn right into the driveway on the right past Dunaway Dr.
*Elevation and mileage are approximate.

Overview: This loop is recommended for equestrians, bikers, and hikers. The trail begins at the Portrero Ridge trailhead. The footing is mainly firm smooth ground with rocks. This is a non-technical loop mainly on single track with moderate hills. **(1)** The Portrero Ridge Tr begins climbing up a few switchbacks and then gradually rides along the ridge 1.2 miles. **(2)** Cross Las Brisas and continue across the street on Sierra Vista Tr 1.4 miles. At the first split stay to the left. Immediately after there is another split so stay to the right and continue up the hill. **(3)** The trail comes out on asphalt. Continue up the asphalt 300 ft. Continue on the left side of the street. Follow the trail sign. **(4)** Cross Rancho Dos Vientos. The Vista Del Mar Tr connects across the street approximately 50 ft west. There is a chain link fence with a 3-ft path of gravel leading to the opening. Follow the trail 1.3 miles as it veers to the right along some houses. Stay to the left at the splits. You will see a fence along Twin Ponds. Its worth stopping to

Sierra Vista Tr

N

take a look. Right at the wooden bridge in between the two ponds. Cross the bridge and stay to the right; there is an entrance into the ponds. **(5)** Back over the bridge. Continue on the Vista Del Mar Tr up a hill .4 mile. **(6)** Take the single track on the right .4 mile. **(7)** Left on Via Ricardo .2 mile. There is a DG path on the side of the road. **(8)** Make a right at the crosswalk on Park View Tr .5 miles. **(9)** The trail spiders at the community park. Travel through the opening in the gate and turn right along the fence leading to Rancho Dos Vientos. **(10)** The trail continues across Rancho Dos Vientos behind the corner house. At the split head up a steep hill to the right on El Rincon Tr .3 mile. **(11)** At the next split turn right .9 mile on El Cerro Tr. **(12)** The trail loops back at the corner of Sierra Vista Tr/Rancho Dos Vientos. Cross Via El Cerro and take Sierra Vista Tr 1.4 miles. **(13)** Continue across Las Brisas on the Portrero Ridge Tr 1.2 miles to the parking lot.

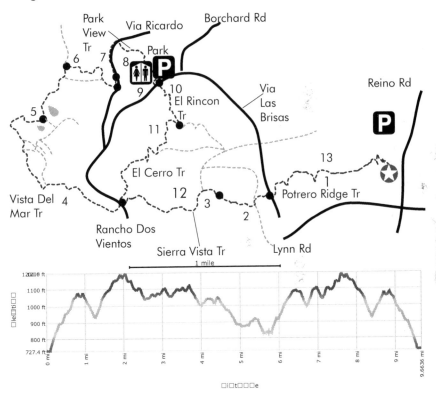

Conejo Mountain Trail

Highlights: Remote; a lot of climbing; views surrounded by volcanic rock and wildflowers in the spring

Miles: 9 miles

Elevation: 1400 ft

Estimated time: biking: 1.5-2 hrs
hiking and horseback riding: 3.5-4 hrs

Technical: ★★★☆☆

Aerobic: ★★★⯪☆

Restrooms: Dos Vientos Community Park

Water: drinking fountain

Dogs: on leash

Parking: parking lot is free

Directions to Trailhead: GPS 34.175684,-118.98173
Dos Vientos Community Park, 4801 Borchard Rd, Newbury Park
101 Fwy north: exit Borchard Rd. South onto Borchard Rd 3.5 miles. The park is on the right side of the street.
101 Fwy south: exit Wendy Dr. South on Wendy Dr 1 mile. Right on Borchard Rd 2 miles. The park is on the right side of the street.
*Elevation and mileage are approximate.

Overview: There is a chance you will see joggers or a mountain biker, but overall this trail is not well traveled. The area is wide open with no shade. The footing is mostly rocky with a moderate grade. There are a few blind turns, but overall there is a clear line of sight. This trail begins at the Dos Vientos Community park with ample parking. **(1)** Follow the dirt path along the fence line that follows Borchard Rd south 300 ft. The trail will hug the park. There is a split in the fence. Make a right going through the split and up the hill behind the park .5 mile on Park View Tr. **(2)** Cross Via Ricardo and continue directly across the street and make a right up the trail. Head north on a single track along side houses with views of farmland for approximately .5 mile. **(3)** The remainder of the trail is wide and has loose rocks as you climb steadily for approximately one mile coming to a junction. **(4)** Right at the junction for 2.5 miles. There is a feeling of isolation and tranquility as the houses are no longer in view. The trail leads to a descent into a canyon with a short ascent up to a beautiful vista with volcanic rock outcroppings with wildflowers in the spring. There are many beautiful places to rest and gaze at the vista along the trail. As the trail continues it weaves among the power

View from the Conejo Mtn Tr

Conejo Mountain Trail

lines and the 101 Freeway comes into view. This trail is a dead end with a locked gate at the bottom near Old Conejo Rd. Return the way you came.

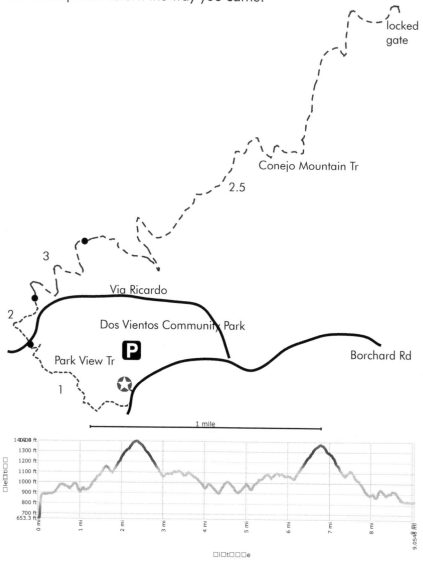

locked gate

Conejo Mountain Tr

2.5

3

Via Ricardo

Dos Vientos Community Park

Park View Tr

Borchard Rd

2

1

1 mile

Satwiwa to Twin Ponds

Highlights:	A walk through a meadow to Twin Ponds with nice views of Camarillo
Miles:	3.5 miles one way
Elevation:	400 ft
Estimated time:	biking: 45 mins-1 hr
	hiking and horseback riding: 2 hrs
Technical:	★★☆☆☆
Aerobic:	★★½☆☆
Restrooms:	in Rancho Sierra Vista/Satwiwa National Park
Water:	drinking fountain
Dogs:	on leash
Parking:	main parking lot, equestrian parking lot - free

Directions to Trailhead: GPS 34.155053,-118.973629
Rancho Sierra Vista/Satwiwa National Park equestrian parking lot, Via Goleta, Newbury Park.
101 Fwy: exit Ventu Park south .6 mile. Right on Lynn Rd 4.2 miles. Left on Via Goleta 300 ft. Right into equestrian parking lot.
*Elevation and mileage are approximate.

Overview: Bikers and hikers may park near the restrooms at the Rancho Sierra Vista/Satwiwa National Park parking lot. Equestrians can park at the equestrian parking lot. Bikers should take Lynn Rd. to the single track because bikes are not allowed on Ranch Overlook Tr. There is street crossing at a crosswalk signal with .4 mile of street travel along a DG path with a fence along the street. The footing is hard packed with some rocks; grade is moderate. This trail begins at Rancho Sierra Vista/Satwiwa Park and skirts along the west end of the Dos Vientos area. **(1)** Begin the single track on the south side of the equestrian parking area. Follow the Ranch Overlook Tr .2 mile. **(2)** At the split veer right through the grassy meadow behind Circle K Stables on the Palomino Tr heading towards Lynn Road 1 mile. **(3)** Cross Lynn Rd at the crosswalk signal and continue west (left) .4 mile along a fence on a dirt path. **(4)** Just before the descent down the Camarillo grade, right on the single track that runs northwest paralleling Rancho Dos Vientos .4 mile. There is a fence to go around with a very short steep hill (10 ft) with approximately 4-5 ft of space in between the fence and the side of the hill. **(5)** When the trail splits, continue in a northwest direction (left) leading to the Vista Del Mar Tr. The fire road is relatively flat and rocky in places with ocean views

Twin Ponds

Satwiwa to Twin Ponds

leading to Twin Ponds 1.3 miles. After the trail makes a right turn at a closed gate there will be a white fence on the right side. The ponds are behind the fence. **(6)** Right turn to cross over the wooden bridge. Follow along the fence on your right. There is a trail leading down to the pond. There is a shady spot over-looking the pond running alongside the trail

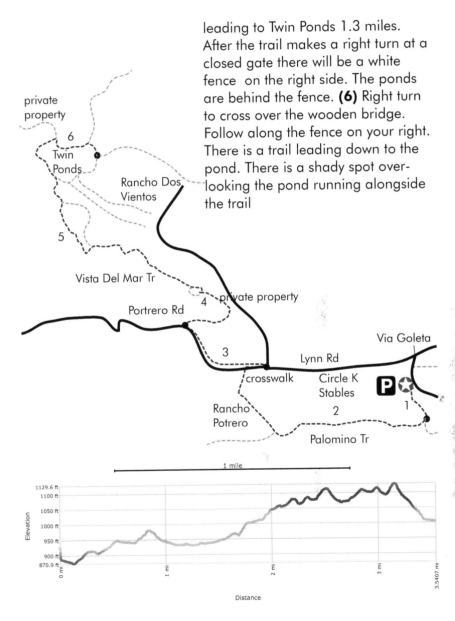

Potrero Ridge Loop

Highlights:	Single track multi area loop linking Los Robles, Rancho Sierra Vista/Satwiwa, and Dos Vientos
Miles:	10 miles
Elevation:	1450 ft
Estimated time:	biking: 1.5+ hrs
	hiking and horseback riding: 4+ hrs
Technical:	★★★☆☆
Aerobic:	★★★☆☆
Restrooms:	Rancho Sierra Vista/Satwiwa main parking lot
Water:	drinking fountain at Rancho Sierra Vista, Portrero Rd. trailhead
Dogs:	on leash
Parking:	street parking is free

Directions to Trailhead: GPS 34.165242,-118.935488
Felton Dr, Newbury Park
101 Fwy: exit Lynn Rd. South on Lynn Rd approximately 3 miles. Left on Felton St .2 mile to the end.
*Elevation and mileage are approximate.

Overview: This ride has street travel on busy streets and many street crossings. The footing is hard ground, loose rocks; the grade is moderate. Park at the cul-de-sac on Felton St at the Los Robles trailhead, **(1)** Travel west for .5 mile toward Wendy Dr. **(2)** Right (north) on Wendy Dr .1 mile. **(3)** Cross the street and begin up Potrero Ridge Fire Rd west with views on both sides .8 mile. **(4)** When the trail begins to descend, right on the short newly cut single track leading to Woodland Oak Ct .2 mile. **(5)** Woodland Oak leads to Reino Rd. Left turn (south) .3 mile. **(6)** After crossing Reino Rd the Potrero Ridge single track climbs up a few switchbacks leading to a gradual climb along the ridgeline on a coastal sage scrub and chaparral lined trail 1.2 miles west. **(7)** The trail gradually descends crossing Via Las Brisas and continues directly across the street on the Sumac and Sierra Vista Trs 1.4 miles west with a few steep hills riding along the ridgeline with views of the ocean. **(8)** The trail continues across Rancho Dos Vientos Dr on Vista Del Mar Tr .1 mile. Go around the chain link **(9)** At the split merge left .4 mile on a single track that runs behind the houses and leads to Lynn Rd. **(10)** Left on Lynn Rd .8 mile. **(11)** Head into the gate of Rancho Sierra Vista/Satwiwa National Park on the right side of the street. **(12)** Take the first single track Broome Tr

Los Robles Tr

Potrero Ridge Loop

approx.100 ft off of Via Goleta on the left side of the street .5 mile.
(13) At the junction right turn .3 mile towards the restrooms and
parking area. **(14)** Continue past the restrooms, drinking fountain,
and continue on the gravel road .3 mile. **(15)** Left on the paved
road .1 mile. **(16)** Right on Wendy Tr 1.2 miles leading to
Potrero/Wendy Dr. **(17)** Right on the Los Robles Connector Tr .5
mile. This single track parallels Potrero Rd with a couple seasonal
creek crossings and lush vegetation **(18)** At the next junction, turn
left. The trail continues directly across the street on Los Robles Tr.
(19) After 1 mile there is a split. Stay straight .3 mile to the left to
Felton St. The trail to the right brings you to Angel Vista.

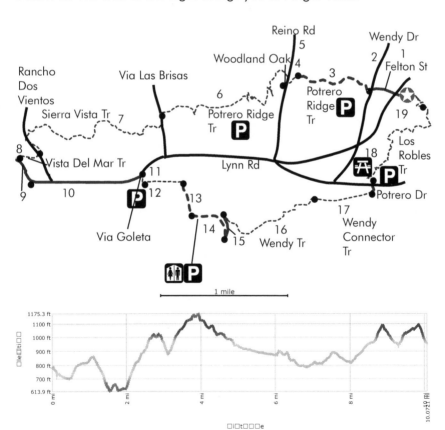

Rancho Sierra Vista/Satwiwa National Park/Point Mugu State Park

Santa Monica Mountains National Park Service
Santa Monica Mountains Conservancy
Santa Monica Mountains National Recreation Area
CA State Parks

Point Mugu State Park and Rancho Sierra Vista/Satwiwa consist of approximately 16,000 acres of rugged landscape, rocky canyons, coastal shrubs, chaparral, oak and sycamore tree savannas, and grassy hillsides. The park includes Rancho Sierra Vista/Satwiwa area at the northwest edge of the park and Point Mugu State Park at the southwest edge of the park a part of the Santa Monica Mountains National Recreation Area. Point Mugu State Park begins at the southern end of Rancho Sierra Vista/Satwiwa area and continues for approximately 8 miles to the coastline and many miles east and west including 5 miles of rugged shoreline and sandy beaches. With approximately 30 miles of fire road and single track multi-use trails, there are many miles of designated hiking trails as well as hiking and horseback riding only trails. The Satwiwa Loop Tr at the north end of the park is a designated hiking only trail. A large amount of protected areas located withing the Santa Monica mountains border the park with trails connecting to open space including Los Robles Open Space, Dos Vientos Open Space, and Circle X Ranch.

The park is a great getaway in a remote location away from civilization. The trails range from non-technical to intermediate ability. There are an assortment of trails, some are flat and wide along a creek with shade; other trails wind up the edge of the mountain with full sun exposure. Be prepared to get your shoes or tires wet at times as there are many seasonal creek crossings.

Big Sycamore Canyon Fire Rd is the main trail connecting the north entrance in Newbury Park and the south entrance on PCH. The trail is approximately 15 ft wide with approximately 3.8 miles of asphalt, and the remainder is dirt with many water crossings. From the north entrance of the park the fire road has a 400-ft descent to the canyon floor. There are many trails spidering off of Big Sycamore Canyon Fire Rd. There are two main entrances to the park. The north entrance located at Rancho Sierra Vista/Satwiwa area off of Goleta Dr in Newbury Park offers free parking. Hours of operation are

Rancho Sierra Vista/Satwiwa National Park/Point Mugu State Park

dawn to dusk. There are restrooms, drinking fountain, and a picnic bench. There is additional parking on the shoulder of Potrero Rd at the Wendy Dr intersection. The south entrance is located at the Point Mugu State Park entrance off of PCH with $8 parking or a CA State Park pass. There are restrooms, a drinking fountain, and showers. Hours of operation are 8 am to 10 pm. There is limited parking along PCH and at Sycamore Cove beach on the south side of PCH, the Ray Miller trailhead, and the Chumash trailhead. Equestrians are not allowed to enter the park from the main Point Mugu entrance off of PCH. Equestrians may enter from the Ray Miller trailhead off of PCH. Equestrians may also enter on Goleta Dr in Newbury Park with parking at the equestrian parking lot. Dogs are not allowed on the backcountry trails. This is a great place to come in the summer time with the ocean breeze. The area also dries well after a rain.

There are water spickets and porta potties along Big Sycamore Canyon Fire Road. Sycamore Campground and Sycamore Beach are located at the south end of the park. Campsites and restrooms are located at the southern end of the trail north of Pacific Coast Hwy. Horse camping is 3.3 and 3.8 miles from the north entrance on Big Sycamore Canyon Trail. There are many Point Mugu State Park Campgrounds. Call 800-444-7275 for detailed information and reservations.

Wendy Tr with views of Boney Mtn

Guadalasca Loop

Highlights:	Scenic climb up switchbacks with lush vegetation ocean views along the ridge; fun descent
Miles:	16.6 miles
Elevation:	2400 ft
Estimated time:	biking: 2-3 hrs hiking and horseback riding: 4-6 hrs
Technical:	★★★ ☆ ☆
Aerobic:	★★★ ☆
Restrooms:	main parking lot, along Big Sycamore Road
Water:	drinking fountains
Dogs:	on leash on paved roads only
Parking:	parking lot is free

Directions to Trailhead: GPS 34.152847,-118.965996
Satwiwa/Rancho Sierra Vista National Park/Point Mugu State Park, Via Goleta, Newbury Park.
101 Fwy: exit Ventu Park. South .6 miles. Right on Lynn Rd 4.2 miles. South on Via Goleta .3 mile to the overflow parking area; and .7 mile to the restrooms and main parking area
*Elevation and mileage are approximate.

Overview: There is also parking on Wendy Dr/Potrero Rd. This loop is a popular mountain biking trail. The footing is firm with rocks and seasonal creek crossings. The area is scenic and the hills are moderate. Equestrians can start from the equestrian parking lot following Ranch Center Rd to Sycamore Cyn Rd. **(1)** Beginning at the main parking area, follow the trail on the west side of the parking lot near the restrooms. Follow the gravel path .3 mile. **(2)** Right on the asphalt road 1.9 miles. The trail travels south toward the ocean beginning with a descent down a paved road and crosses a wooden bridge that takes you to the valley floor of the park. Big Sycamore Canyon Fireroad is lined with sycamore trees providing partial shade. **(3)** Right on Ranch Center Rd 2.3 miles on the old paved road. The road climbs up a hill and descends down by an old shed joining Wood Cyn Tr. **(4)** Follow Wood Cyn Tr north 1.3 miles through the seasonal water crossings. The trail is wide, although poison oak encroaches onto the trail. **(5)** Right on Guadalasca Tr 2.6 miles. Guadalasca is a moderate scenic rocky single track that gently climbs up the northern edge of the hillside. **(6)** Once you've reached the top, the trail turns into Overlook Tr. Continue on Overlook Tr

View from the top of Guadalasca looking towards Camarillo

Sin Nombre Tr with horses in the background

Guadalasca Loop

descending down the hill 1.3 miles. You will pass one junction on the left. **(7)** The next junction on the left is Wood Cyn Vista Tr (Backbone Tr) 1.8 miles. This is a fun single track that descends gradually with sweeping turns intersecting with Big Sycamore Cyn Fire Road. **(8)** Left on the fire road .1 mile. **(9)** Left on the next fire road .1 mile. **(10)** Right on Two Foxes Tr 1.5 miles. **(11)** At the split stay to the left on Sin Nombre .9 mile. Two Foxes and Sin Nombre trails are relatively flat single track trails that parallel Big Sycamore Cyn Fire Rd and meander through meadows and grasslands. **(12)** Right on Ranch Center Rd. .3 mile. **(13)** Left on Big Sycamore Cyn Fire Rd1.9 miles along the valley floor and up the asphalt hill. **(14)** Left on the trail.3 mile leading back to the parking area.

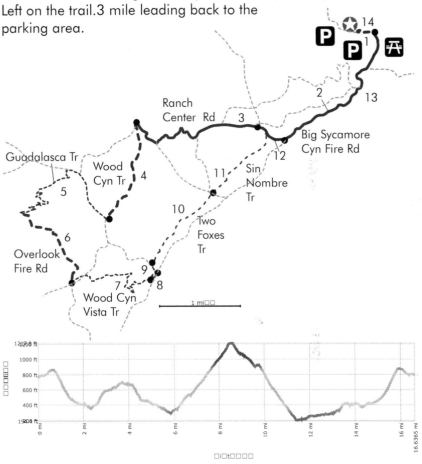

Scenic Overlook Trail Loop 🚲 🥾 🐎

Highlights:	Scenic trail; climb up a fireroad with ocean views; descend down twisty single track
Miles:	10 miles
Elevation:	1000 ft
Estimated time:	biking: 1-1.5 hrs hiking and horseback riding: 2-3 hrs
Technical:	★★★ ☆ ☆
Aerobic:	★★★ ☆ ☆
Restrooms:	yes
Water:	drinking fountain
Dogs:	no
Parking:	parking lot is $8 at the park entrance; limited free parking on PCH

Directions to Trailhead: GPS 34.071742,-119.013251
Point Mugu State Park, 9000 W PCH, Malibu
101 Fwy: exit 55 For Las Posas Rd. Left on Las Posas Rd 1 mile. Straight to continue on S Las Posas Rd 6.5 miles. Left on PCH south 4.3 miles. Destination is on the left.
*Elevation and mileage are approximate.

Overview: Horses are not allowed at the Point Mugu entrance; horses can take the Ray Miller Tr to Overlook Tr. The footing is mainly firm and smooth with a rocky downhill with a moderate grade. **(1)** Follow the flat partially shaded trail north on Big Sycamore Cyn Fire Rd .4 mile to the Overlook Fire Rd. **(2)** Left on the Overlook Fire Rd as it skirts the edge of the hill along the mountain top at a moderate grade 4.7 miles with full sun exposure and beautiful views of Boney Peak and Big Sycamore Cyn. The trail is scenic the entire time. When the trail begins the descent, keep an eye out on the right side for Wood Cyn Vista (Backbone) Trail sign. **(3)** Right on the trail as you head east down the hill 1.8 miles with areas of lush vegetation and coastal sage scrub. The Backbone Tr is semi-technical with a few switchbacks and rocks to maneuver over. Occasionally there is water at the bottom of the trail just before the trail joins Sycamore Cyn Fire Rd. **(4)** South (right) along the valley floor 3 miles among the forest of Sycamore trees leading back to PCH.

Overlook Tr

Scenic Overlook Trail Loop

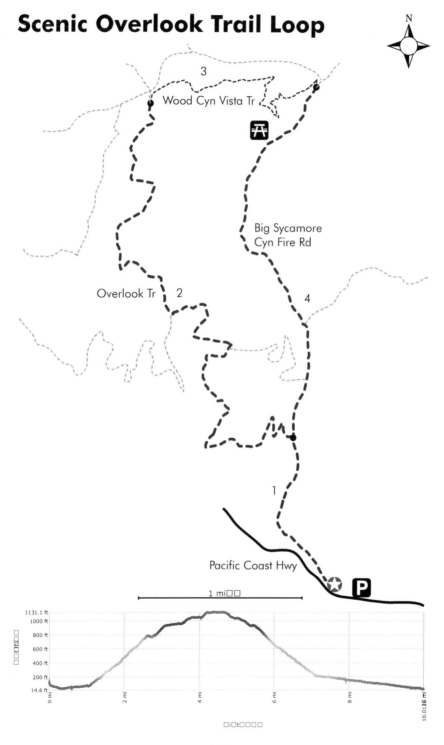

N

Wood Cyn Vista Tr

3

Big Sycamore
Cyn Fire Rd

Overlook Tr   2

4

1

Pacific Coast Hwy

1 mi

1131.1 ft
1000 ft
800 ft
600 ft
400 ft
200 ft
14.6 ft

0 mi
2 mi
4 mi
6 mi
8 mi
10.01 mi

Upper Sycamore Canyon Loop 🦶 🏇

Highlights:	Stroll through the forest, across streams, and along the creek leading to panoramic views
Miles:	5.6 miles
Elevation:	950 ft
Estimated time:	hiking and horseback riding: 2 hrs
Technical:	★★★✦☆
Aerobic:	★★★✦☆
Restrooms:	yes
Water:	drinking fountain
Dogs:	no
Parking:	parking lot is free

Directions to Trailhead: GPS 34.155071,-118.973624
Rancho Sierra Vista/Satwiwa National Park equestrian parking lot, Via Goleta, Newbury Park.
101 Fwy north: exit Ventu Park. South on Ventu Park .6 miles. Right on Lynn Rd 4.2 miles. Left on Via Goleta .1 mile to the equestrian parking lot and .7 mile to the main parking area.
*Elevation and mileage are approximate.

Overview: Most of this trail is for hikers and equestrians. Bikes are allowed on Sycamore Canyon Fire Rd and Broome Trail. Bikes are not allowed on Upper Sycamore Canyon Tr, Old Boney Tr, or Ranch Overlook Tr. This trail begins at the equestrian parking lot or the main parking lot. The footing varies from asphalt to firm with rocks. This trail can be ridden in either direction. **(1)** Cross Via Goleta; turn left for 200 ft. Just before leaving the gates of the park turn right to enter the Broome trail .7 mile. The trail drops down a hill and bends to the right. **(2)** Cross Via Goleta and continue on the flat gravely trail that passes the restrooms and main parking area .4 miles. **(3)** Right on Big Sycamore Cyn Rd 1 mile. The asphalt road descends 400 ft leading to the shady valley floor. The ascent down Big Sycamore Cyn Fire Rd can be quite crowded on the weekends and holidays with mountain bikers, hikers, and equestrians. **(4)** 200 ft after crossing the bridge, there is a porta potty next to the Upper Sycamore Tr. Left on Upper Sycamore Tr 1.3 miles. This single track trail meanders through a lush forest and crosses a seasonal stream many times gradually climbing the canyon. The trail is hard packed with a few rock steps. There can be strands of poison oak lining the trail. The trail intersects with Old Boney Tr West.

Upper Sycamore Cyn Fire Rd

Upper Sycamore Canyon Loop

(5) Left on Old Boney Tr .9 mile. The footing is firm, uneven, and rocky. This is an active trail so you can expect to see many hikers. There is a bench at the top of the hill offering a lovely view. **(6)** Left at the first intersection leading to Big Sycamore Cyn Rd. **(7)** Right on the asphalt road 300 ft. Take the Ranch Overlook Tr on the left side of the road 1.2 miles to the equestrian parking lot or .9 mile to the main parking lot.

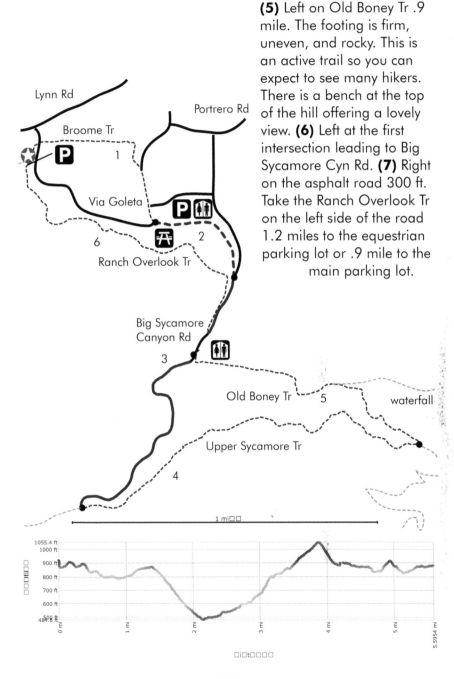

Danielson Monument– Old Boney Trail

Highlights:	Travel past a waterfall under shaded sycamore trees gradually descending through a chaparral lined trail with panoramic views
Miles:	7.7 miles
Elevation:	1600 ft
Estimated time:	hiking and horseback riding: 2.5+hrs
Technical:	★★★✦☆
Aerobic:	★★★✦☆
Restrooms:	yes
Water:	drinking fountain
Dogs:	no
Parking:	parking lot is free

Directions to Trailhead: GPS 34.155071,-118.973624
Via Goleta, Rancho Sierra Vista National Park, Newbury Park
101 Fwy: exit 46 Ventu Park toward Newbury Park. South on Ventu Park .6 mile. Right on Lynn Rd 4.2 miles. Left on Via Goleta .1 mile to the equestrian parking lot and .7 mile to the main parking area.
*Elevation and mileage are approximate.

Overview: Hikers can also begin from Wendy Dr/ Potrero Rd. This route is for hikers and equestrians. This loop is very scenic. The footing is uneven and rocky in places. The grade is moderate. The trail narrows and can be on an edge at times past the Danielson Monument. Just past the monument, Old Boney Tr has low hanging trees. If you are on horseback, dismounting and hand walking or ducking are all an options; or turn around. The trail will be crowded to this point. Once you pass the Danielson Monument, the crowds suddenly disappear. This route begins at the equestrian parking lot that passes by the main parking area. Hikers may begin at the main parking lot on Via Goleta. **(1)** Cross Via Goleta, and turn left for 200 ft. Just before leaving the gates of the park turn right to enter Broome Tr .7 mile. The trail drops down a hill and bends to the right. **(2)** Cross Via Goleta and continue on the flat gravely trail that passes the restrooms and main parking area .4 mile. **(3)** Right on the pavement approximately 20 ft. Follow Ranch Overlook Tr .2 mile, then head south and parallel the pavement. **(4)** Cross the pavement just before the trail drops down to the canyon and left on Old Boney Tr.

Danielson Monument–
Old Boney Trail

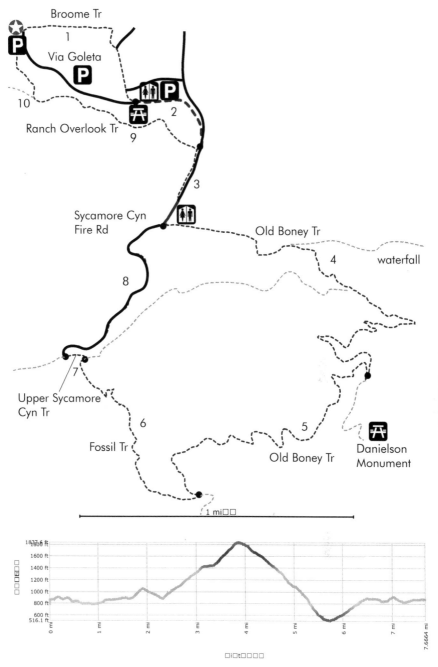

Broome Tr

1

Via Goleta

10

Ranch Overlook Tr

9

2

3

Sycamore Cyn
Fire Rd

Old Boney Tr

4

waterfall

8

7

Upper Sycamore
Cyn Tr

6

5

Fossil Tr

Old Boney Tr

Danielson
Monument

1 mi

Danielson Monument– Old Boney Trail

The trail is rocky in places with a moderate grade. Follow Old Boney Tr keeping right at the next two junctions. The trail descends down the canyon, crosses a seasonal water crossing, and continues climbing up the canyon through the sycamore forest and along the edge of the mountain for 2 miles. There is a short trail that leads to a seasonal waterfall. Horses are not allowed on this trail. Old Boney Tr continues to climb for the majority of the trail with vista viewpoints along the way. **(5)** At the Danielson Monument junction, right on Old Boney Tr or left will take you to the Danielson Monument after .3 mile. Hikers can continue for many miles past the cabin site, although the trail becomes very rocky with boulder climbing and is not open to horses. Danielson has a picnic bench and shade to enjoy your rest. Continuing on, follow Old Boney Tr. climbing up the hill 1.4 miles. There are a couple viewspots along the way for a nice photo opportunity. The trail is not always maintained. Low hanging chaparral branches line the trail. Horseback riders may need to duck for approximately .75 mile. The trail will begin to ascend leading to Fossil Tr junction. **(6)** Right on Fossil Tr .9 mile. This trail can be steep in sections, narrow, and on the edge. If you don't want to take the pavement up the hill then from Fossil Tr turn right on Upper Sycamore Cyn Tr to Old Boney. Left on Old Boney and continue the way you came. **(7)** Left at the next junction on Upper Sycamore Cyn Tr .1 mile. **(8)** Right on Sycamore Cyn Fire Rd. Cross over the big wooden bridge and head up the pavement .8 mile. **(9)** Left on Ranch Overlook Tr 1.2 miles. **(10)** Right at the split leading back to the parking lot.

Old Boney Tr

Ray Miller Trail

Highlights:	Gradual switchbacks climbing up a canyon with ocean and coastline views
Miles:	2.8 miles one way
Elevation:	1200 ft
Estimated time:	hiking & horseback riding: 2 hrs
Technical:	★★☆☆☆
Aerobic:	★★★⯪☆
Restrooms:	no
Water:	drinking fountain
Dogs:	no
Parking:	parking lot is $8

Directions to Trailhead: GPS 34.086676,-119.036973
La Jolla Cyn, Pacific Coast Hwy, Malibu
.5 mile north of Point Mugu State Park entrance
101 Fwy: exit 55 for Las Posas Rd .4 mile. Left on N Las Posas Rd 1 mile. Straight onto S. Las Posas Rd 6.5 miles. Left on S. PCH 4 miles.
*Elevation and mileage are approximate.

Top of Ray Miller Tr.

Ray Miller Trail

N

Overview:

This is one of the most spectacular trails with an ocean view the entire time. The trail is on the edge of the hill. After a rain sections of the trail may wash out. The trail is narrow with smooth footing most of the time and a couple rocky sections with a moderate grade. This is a popular trail with hikers. Its best to do this trail when the sun is shining to enjoy the view. **(1)** Begin at the La Jolla Cyn parking lot. Walk toward the informational kiosk, continue across the street and you'll see a sign "Backbone-Ray Miller Tr." The trail passes by restrooms approximately .5 mile from the start at the campground. Follow the trail 2.8 miles to the Overlook Tr. The Overlook Tr connects from PCH at the Sycamore Campground up the mountain towards La Jolla Cyn. This fire road is very picturesque. Hikers can make a loop making a left (north) on Overlook Tr to La Jolla Cyn Tr back to the parking lot. La Jolla Cyn Tr is a hiking only trail. Equestrians can make a loop by making a right on Overlook Tr and continuing down to Big Sycamore Fire Rd. Left on the fire road. Left on Fireline Tr and a right back up Overlook Tr and a left back down Ray Miller Tr.

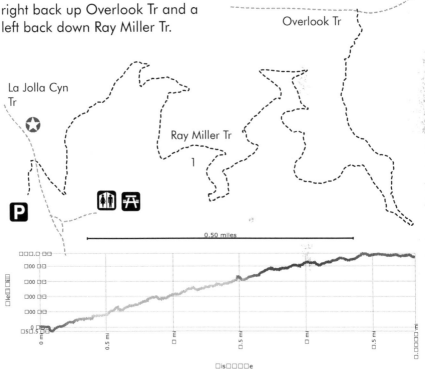

Overlook Tr

La Jolla Cyn Tr

Ray Miller Tr

1

0.50 miles

Conejo Canyons/Hill Canyon

COSCA
City of Thousand Oaks
Conejo Recreation and Park District
Ventura County Parks Department

Conejo Canyons is located Santa Rosa Valley with approximately 1,600 acres of deeply eroded canyons, grassy meadows, spectacular views, oak woodlands, and riparian habitats. The area is usually a bit cooler than other areas of the Conejo Valley. Conejo Canyons is in a remote location that makes for a nice getaway. Since the new bridge has been constructed, the area has become more popular and is now suitable for hiking, horseback riding, and mountain biking. Conejo Canyons is adjacent to and connects to Wildwood Park and Arroyo Conejo. The Hill Canyon Trail connects to Arroyo Conejo. It is an excellent option for a hot day with many water crossings on a flat trail along riparian woodlands. The Canyon Overlook Trail leads directly to Wildwood up a steep rocky trail for almost one mile. Parking is free at the moment, but it will cost $2 at the Santa Rosa County Park parking lot. The area is accessible from 7 am to 7:30 pm. Accommodations include restrooms, drinking fountains, two arenas, and hitching posts near the picnic tables.

Conejo Cyns

Conejo Canyons to Wildwood Park Loop

Highlights: Very scenic; rocky switcbacks up Mount Clef through Wildwood, and return on a flat trail in Arroyo Conejo with many water crossings

Miles: 8.2 miles

Elevation: 1450 ft

Estimated time: biking: 1.5-2 hrs
hiking and horseback riding: 4 hrs

Technical: ★★★☆☆

Aerobic: ★★★☆☆

Restrooms: yes

Water: drinking fountain

Dogs: on leash

Parking: parking lot is $2

Directions to Trailhead: GPS 34.226449,-118.930264
10241 Hill Canyon Rd, Santa Rosa Valley
23 Fwy: exit 19 for Tierra Rejada Rd. West on Tierra Rejada Rd .5 mile. South on Moorpark Rd 1.5 miles. Right (west) on Santa Rosa Rd 3.7 miles. Left on Hill Cyn Rd .3 mile.
*Elevation and mileage are approximate.

Crossing the water in Wildwood

Conejo Canyons to Wildwood Park Loop

Overview: This loop is good for hiking, horseback riding, and mountain biking. Begin in Hill Cyn; go through Wildwood; and continue back along Arroyo Conejo Tr. You will get your feet wet on this ride because many creek crossings do not have bridges yet. There are a few blind turns and rocky sections. The hills are moderate with a couple steep hills. There is a very high step over (2-ft.) at the end of Lynnmere Tr. Riders may need to dismount and lead the horse over it. Begin at the Santa Rosa County Park parking lot. **(1)** The trail begins alongside the fence and crosses Hill Cyn at the new bridge. Go over both step overs and head up Canyon Overlook Tr. – a steep rocky hill .8 mile to the top of Mount Clef Ridge. **(2)** Left along the newly cut trail .8 mile along the edge of the ridge with a moderate grade. This is a brand new trail and the dirt is soft. This trail runs into the Lizard Rock Tr. **(3)** Left on Lizard Rock Tr .2 mile in Wildwood Park. **(4)** Left on the Mesa Tr .5 mile. **(5)** Right down N. Tepee Tr .5 mile. **(6)** Left at the Tepee Tr. Left at the tepee .1 mile. **(7)** Cross Wildwood Cyn Tr and continue straight on the Lynnmere Tr crossing the water. The trail continues uphill on the Lynnmere Tr .5 mile. **(8)** Left at the wooden bridge and continue on the Lynnmere Tr .7 mile. **(9)** At the split take a right turn and go around the houses and cross Lynnmere St. **(10)** The trail continues across the street. When the trail splits, stay to the right where the trail drops down the technical section of Lynnmere Tr .7 mile. **(11)** You are now in between houses. In 300 ft the Lynnmere Tr continues to the right. **(12)** Turn left along the houses and descend for .4 mile connecting to the Arroyo Conejo Tr. **(13)** Right on the trail 1.2 miles on a flat trail with many water crossings. The bridges may wash away. Some of the rocks in the water for crossing are unstable. **(14)** After passing the water treatment plant you'll go through another water crossing and up a hill. There is a single track on the right side of the hill about 30 ft. up the hill. Right on the single track .3 mile to a junction. **(15)** Straight through the junction. The last water crossing is deep. It is 1.1 miles to the deep water crossing. To avoid the water go over the bridge. Make a right after .9 mile over the bridge, left turn to the parking lot.

Conejo Canyons to Wildwood Park Loop

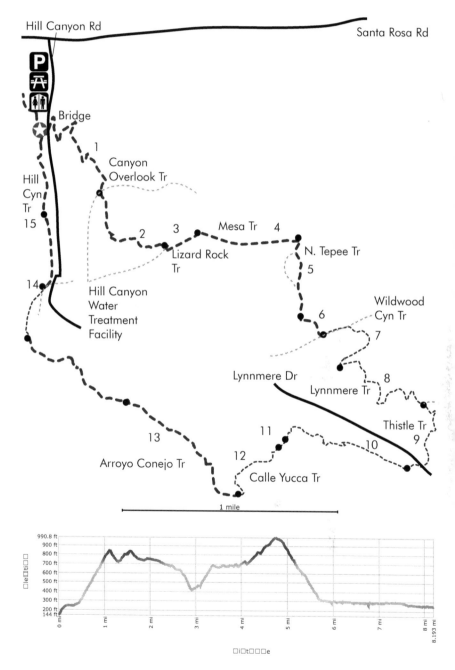

Hill Canyon Rd

Santa Rosa Rd

P

Bridge

Hill Cyn Tr

15

1

Canyon Overlook Tr

14

Hill Canyon Water Treatment Facility

2

3

Lizard Rock Tr

Mesa Tr

4

N. Tepee Tr

5

6

Wildwood Cyn Tr

7

Lynnmere Dr

Lynnmere Tr

8

Thistle Tr

9

10

13

11

12

Arroyo Conejo Tr

Calle Yucca Tr

1 mile

990.8 ft
900 ft
800 ft
700 ft
600 ft
500 ft
400 ft
300 ft
200 ft
144 ft

0 mi
1 mi
2 mi
3 mi
4 mi
5 mi
6 mi
7 mi
8.193 mi

Hill Canyon Trail/
Hawk Canyon Loop

Highlights:	Peaceful; spectacular views on the grassy vista
Miles:	5.1 miles
Elevation:	500 ft
Estimated time:	biking: 1 hr
	hiking and horseback riding: 1.5-2 hrs
Technical:	★★☆☆☆
Aerobic:	★★★☆☆
Restrooms:	yes
Water:	drinking fountain
Dogs:	on leash
Parking:	parking lot - free

Directions to Trailhead: GPS 34.226449,-118.930264
10241 Hill Canyon Rd, Santa Rosa Valley
23 Fwy: exit 19 for Tierra Rejada Rd. West on Tierra Rejada Rd .5 mile. South on Moorpark Rd 1.5 miles. Right (west) on Santa Rosa Rd 3.7 miles. Left on Hill Cyn Rd .3 mile.
*Elevation and mileage are approximate.

Overview: This trail is good for horseback riding, hiking, and mountain biking. The footing is firm and smooth with many rocky areas, the hills are moderate. There is little shade. **(1)** This trail can begin either crossing the bridge or through the water crossing. The trails run parallel alongside the creek .1 mile. **(2)** After the trails merge, follow the Hill Cyn Tr .9 mile to the intersection. The trail is flat and wide with a creek and a beautiful meadow. **(3)** Right on Western Plateau Tr 1.5 miles. The trail is rocky in places with cactus and grassy meadows on both sides with nice views. **(4)** You will come to an intersection with many turnoffs. Continue straight on the trail that takes a slight left .7 mile down the fire road. **(5)** Just before the fire road starts climbing uphill there is a single track on the left. Follow Hawk Cyn Tr .4 mile. It is very easy to miss. The trail runs along the creek with some poison oak alongside the trail. There are a couple little creek crossings. The trail takes a sudden left turn down a hill and across a creek. **(6)** Follow the trail up the hill and take the slight right .6 mile to an intersection. The trail you went up should be on your left side looking up the hill. **(7)** At the intersection, left turn 1 mile to the bridge or continue past the

Conejo Cyns

Hill Cyn Trail/Hawk Cyn Loop

Santa Rosa Rd

bridge to cross the deep water crossing leading to the parking lot.

1

Hill Cyn Tr

5

Western Plateau Tr

2

Hill Cyn Rd

4

Hawk Cyn Tr

3

1 mile

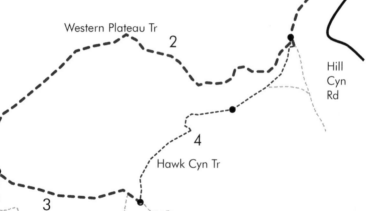

Corriganville Park

Rancho Simi Open Space Conservation Agency
Rancho Simi Recreation and Park District
City of Simi Valley

Nestled at the northern end of Simi Valley on the south side of the 118 Freeway, Corriganville Park has over four miles of multi-use trails meandering through the 205 acre nature preserve. Corriganville Park's trail system connects to Chatsworth and Rocky Peak Park. The sandstone peaks, year-round stream, and oak forest make this area a wonderful place to explore. Ammenities include shaded picnic tables, portable toilets with soap and water, a horse water trough, drinking fountain, archery, and a large dirt parking lot with ample room for parking. There are train tracks alongside Smith Rd near the parking lot and the Interpretive Tr. Hours of operation are dawn to dusk and closed for inclement weather. Corriganville Park was an old movie ranch where over 3500 movies, television shows, and commercials were filmed.

Interpretive Tr Rest Area

Lower Stagecoach Trail/ 🚲 🥾 🐎
Rocky Peak Trail/Chumash Trail

Highlights:	Scenic, technical, strenuous trail with switchbacks on the old Stagecoach Tr; climb up Rocky Peak; fun descent down Chumash Tr
Miles:	8.2 miles
Elevation:	2000 ft
Estimated time:	mountain biking: 2+hrs
	hiking and horseback riding: 4+hrs
Technical:	★★★★☆
Aerobic:	★★★★☆
Restrooms:	porta potty
Water:	horse water trough, drinking fountain
Dogs:	on leash
Parking:	dirt parking lot is free

Directions to Trailhead: GPS 34.264325,-118.652679
Smith Rd, Corriganville Park Simi Valley
118 Fwy: exit 30 for Kuehner Dr. North on Kuehner Dr 1.1 miles. Left on Smith Rd .4 mile. Destination is on the left.
*Elevation and mileage are approximate.

Overview: There is little shade on this ride. There are approximately 3 miles of street riding to connect back to Corriganville Park. This trail begins on the historic Stagecoach Tr. The trail is narrow with many ups and downs meandering through sandstone peaks. Equestrians can ride the trail until it reaches Santa Susana Pass Rd. There is .2 mile of street riding on Santa Susana Pass Rd with no shoulder leading to Rocky Peak Park. **(1)** Begin on the flat wide Interpretive Tr at the end of the parking lot .3 mile. Pass the bathrooms and picnic area and head toward the freeway. The trail climbs a few steep switchbacks .3 mile then branches off to the right .4 mile. **(2)** Left on Santa Susana Pass Rd .2 mile. **(3)** Left on Rocky Peak Rd .1 mile. Go over the freeway and continue up the fire road 3.8 miles. The fire road is steep, rocky, in full sun, but very scenic. The trail climbs the ridge with panoramic views; you will pass beautiful sandstone formations. This trail can be crowded on the weekends. **(4)** Left down Chumash Tr 2.6 miles for downhill fun rolling over boulders and passing through caves. This trail comes out at Flannagan Dr. Stay on the trail alongside Flannagan Dr .7 mile

Lower Stagecoach Trail/ Rocky Peak Trail/ Chumash Trail

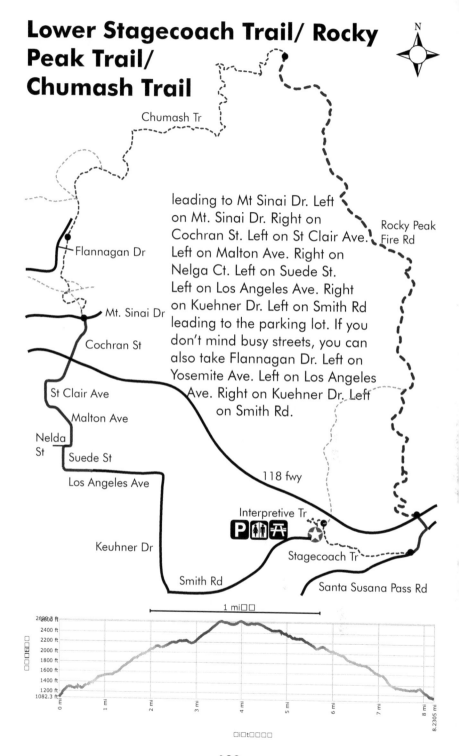

N

Chumash Tr

leading to Mt Sinai Dr. Left on Mt. Sinai Dr. Right on Cochran St. Left on St Clair Ave. Left on Malton Ave. Right on Nelga Ct. Left on Suede St. Left on Los Angeles Ave. Right on Kuehner Dr. Left on Smith Rd leading to the parking lot. If you don't mind busy streets, you can also take Flannagan Dr. Left on Yosemite Ave. Left on Los Angeles Ave. Right on Kuehner Dr. Left on Smith Rd.

Rocky Peak Fire Rd

Flannagan Dr

Mt. Sinai Dr

Cochran St

St Clair Ave

Malton Ave

Nelda St

Suede St

Los Angeles Ave

118 fwy

Interpretive Tr

Keuhner Dr

Stagecoach Tr

Smith Rd

Santa Susana Pass Rd

1 mi

2600 ft
2400 ft
2200 ft
2000 ft
1800 ft
1600 ft
1400 ft
1200 ft
1082.3 ft

0 mi · 1 mi · 2 mi · 3 mi · 4 mi · 5 mi · 6 mi · 7 mi · 8 mi · 8.2305 mi

Interpretive Tr leading to switchbacks

Upper Stagecoach Trail/ Rocky Peak Trailhead

Highlights:	Scenic; technical trail with switchbacks on the old Stagecoach Tr; panoramic views
Miles:	2.8 miles one way
Elevation:	1288 ft
Estimated time:	mountain biking: 1+hrs hiking and horseback riding: 1.5+hrs
Technical:	★★★★☆
Aerobic:	★★★★☆
Restrooms:	porta potty
Water:	horse water trough, drinking fountain
Dogs:	on leash
Parking:	dirt parking lot is free

Directions to Trailhead: GPS 34.264325,-118.652679
Smith Rd, Corriganville Park Simi Valley
118 Fwy: exit 30 for Kuehner Dr. North on Kuehner Dr 1.1 miles. Left on Smith Rd .4 mile. Destination is on the left.
*Elevation and mileage are approximate.

Overview: There is little shade on this ride. This trail is suitable for hikers, sure-footed horses, and intermediate/ advanced mountain bikers. It's a wonder how wagons used to maneuver on these narrow trails with many ups and downs meandering through sandstone peaks. There is a street crossing at Santa Susana Rd with .1 mile on Lilac Ln. (a neighborhood street) connecting the Stagecoach Tr. After crossing the street the trail comes out on a mesa with an overlook of the valley. There are a couple sections where the trail is steep and rutted. The footing is varied— firm, loose, and shaley. **(1)** Begin on the flat wide Interpretive Tr at the end of the parking lot .3 mile. Pass the bathrooms and picnic area and head toward the freeway. **(2)** Take the trail on the left as it climbs a few steep switchbacks .3 mile. **(3)** At the junction, branch off to the right .4 mile. **(4)** Cross Santa Susana Rd and connect directly to Lilac Ln a quiet neighborhood street .1 mile. On the left you will see a dirt lot with a kiosk. This is another trailhead. **(5)** The Stagecoach Tr to the left will also lead to Santa Susana Pass Rd but it is not the right way. Go around the gate and head east. Stay to the left at the next two splits. You will end up to the left of the power lines.

Mesa on Upper Stagecoach Tr

Upper Stagecoach Trail/ Rocky Peak Trailhead

The trail drops up and down a couple hills leading to a mesa over-looking the valley. This is a nice place to turn around to avoid narrow drop offs and street travel with no shoulder **(6)** To continue left at the split leading to Santa Susana Pass Rd .5 mile. This section of the trail is narrow and has a few drop offs. **(7)** Left .2 mile on Santa Susana Pass Rd, then right over the freeway to Rocky Peak trailhead.

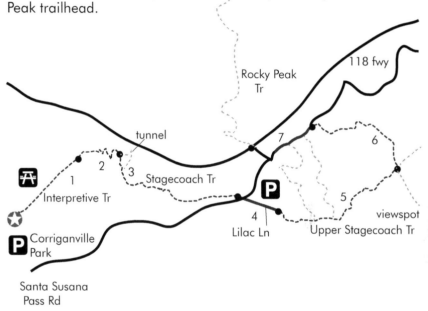

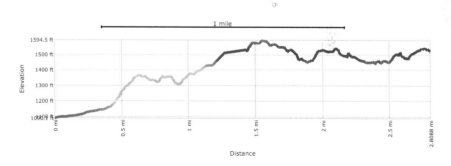

Rocky Peak Park/ Marr Ranch Parkland

Rancho Simi Park and Recreation
Santa Monica Mountains Conservancy

Located in the Santa Susana Mountains of 4,800 acres nestled in the eastern end of Simi Valley on the northern side of the 118 Freeway. The caves, massive sandstone formations, and oak savannahs in the Rocky Peak Park are spectacular. This area is suitable for mountain bike riders, hikers, and equestrians.

There is some street travel involved when making many of the loops in the area. The 6.5 mile Rocky Peak Tr is the main fire road that begins at the 118 freeway and climbs rapidly 1450 ft along the ridge line heading north. The tread is hard packed with rocks, some steep, rutted sections, and a couple sandy patches. The fire road ascends on the ridge for 6.5 miles connecting to Las Llajas Cyn Tr, Chumash Tr, Johnson Mtwy, and Hummingbird Tr. The single track trails range in technical ability from intermediate to advanced. Johnson Mtwy is the least technical trail beginning in Chatsworth ascending 3.3 miles with 1400 ft elevation leading to the northern end of Rocky Peak Fire Road. Chumash Tr is located at the west end of the area with a 2.6 mile single track trail beginning at the end of Flannagan Dr climbing 1100 ft elevation leading to the northern end of Rocky Peak Fire Rd. The majority of the trail is steep and towards the last half mile, the trail gets steeper with several technical challenges. Hummingbird Tr can be accessed from Rocky Peak Fire Road .75 mile from the base of Rocky Peak Park entrance and ends at Keuhner Dr at the 118 freeway. The trail is 2.3 miles long and very technical. This trail is for advanced riders only. There is slick rock riding, sharp switchbacks, steep sections, and many rocky sections.

The Las Llajas Fire Rd. is recommended for horses and novice mountain bikers wanting to enjoy a pleasant stroll along the valley floor through the riparian woodlands partially shaded from oak trees for 3.5 miles with a 775 ft elevation gain round trip. Tapo Canyon Open Space has wide semi-shaded sandy trails leading to a narrow single track traversing up and down the canyon with little shade. Street parking is available on Yosemite Dr. to access Las Llajas Cyn Tr. There is a small dirt parking lot on Tapo Canyon Rd with access to Tapo Canyon Open Space for the Chivos Canyon Trail. Much of this area dries quickly after a rain.

Tapo Canyon Loop

Highlights: Non-technical, peaceful getaway on a moderate grade through the oak trees

Miles: 4.4 miles

Elevation: 750 ft

Estimated time: mountain biking: 30 mins-1 hr
hiking & horseback riding:1-1.5 hrs

Technical: ★★ ☆ ☆ ☆

Aerobic: ★★½ ☆ ☆

Restrooms: no

Water: no

Dogs: on leash

Parking: dirt parking lot is free

Directions to Trailhead: GPS 34.304751,-118.720354
Tapo Canyon Rd, Simi Valley
118 Fwy: exit 27 for Tapo Canyon Rd. Head north on Tapo Canyon Rd approximately 1.5 miles. There is a "dip 35 mph" sign approx. 10 ft before the parking area on the right side.
*Elevation and mileage are approximate.

Tapo Cyn Open Space

Tapo Canyon Loop
Overview:

The parking lot is a small, dirt lot with a wide apron at the entrance. If you are driving a horse trailer, you may need to back the trailer into the parking lot. There is not enough room to turn around. This trail is wide most of the time with firm smooth ground and many sandy sections. **(1)** Cross the first stepover and make a left 1.3 miles on the moderate trail along the partially shaded trail. The footing is firm with sandy patches. **(2)** At the junction, head left up a steep hill .2 mile. **(3)** At the next intersection go straight through on the single track heading downhill .9 mile.

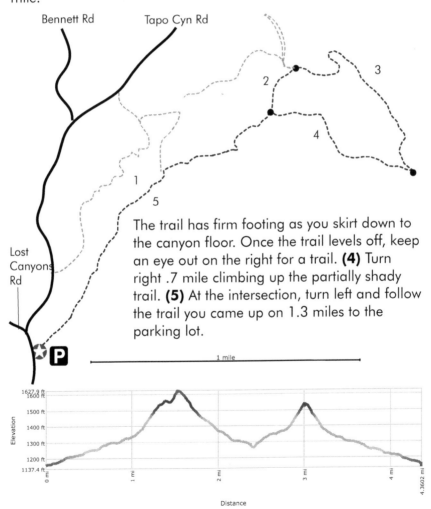

The trail has firm footing as you skirt down to the canyon floor. Once the trail levels off, keep an eye out on the right for a trail. **(4)** Turn right .7 mile climbing up the partially shady trail. **(5)** At the intersection, turn left and follow the trail you came up on 1.3 miles to the parking lot.

Tapo Canyon/ Chivos Canyon Loop

Highlights:	Peaceful getaway with a moderate grade through the oak trees leading to single track climbing up Chivos Cyn
Miles:	7.5 miles
Elevation:	1550 ft
Estimated time:	mountain biking: 1-1.5 hrs
	hiking and horseback riding: 1.5-2 hrs
Technical:	★★★☆☆
Aerobic:	★★★☆☆
Restrooms:	no
Water:	no
Dogs:	on leash
Parking:	dirt parking lot is free

Directions to Trailhead: GPS34.304751,-118.720354
Tapo Canyon Rd. Simi Valley
118 Fwy: exit 27 for Tapo Canyon Rd. Head north on Tapo Canyon Rd approximately 1.5 miles. There is a "dip 35 mph" sign 10 ft before the parking area on the right side.
*Elevation and mileage are approximate.

Overview: This ride has some shade. The parking lot is a small, dirt lot with a wide apron at the entrance. If you are driving a horse trailer, you will need to back the trailer up. There is not enough room to turn around. This trail begins wide with sand sections, cross a wash leading to a narrow single track climbing up the canyon with a moderate grade and smooth firm footing. The trail is off camber at times with a drop on one side. **(1)** Take the trail to the left 1.3 miles on the moderate trail along the partially shaded trail. The footing is smooth with sandy patches. **(2)** At the junction, head left up a steep hill .2 mile. **(3)** At the next intersection go straight through on the single track heading downhill 1.2 miles. **(4)** Once the trail levels off, the trail comes to a T. Left on Chivos Cyn Tr 1.4 miles on a single track winding up the trail. There is an old rusty piece of metal on the side of the trail that you need to maneuver around. There are a few short steep sections. **(5)** When the trail levels off at the top of the hill, right at the intersection .3 mile. **(6)** You should be able to see a trail to the right going uphill. After 20 yards

Chivos Cyn Tr

Tapo Cyn Open Space

Tapo Canyon/
Chivos Canyon Loop

turn right. The trail is overgrown and hard to see. After .1 mile you will pass an old water tank. Continue down the hill .3 mile connecting back to the beginning of Chivos Cyn Tr. **(7)** Left on Chivos Cyn Tr .4 mile. **(8)** At the next intersection, right .3 mile returning through the trees. **(9)** When the trail splits, turn right .7 mile climbing through the oak trees. **(10)** At the intersection, turn left and follow the trail you came up

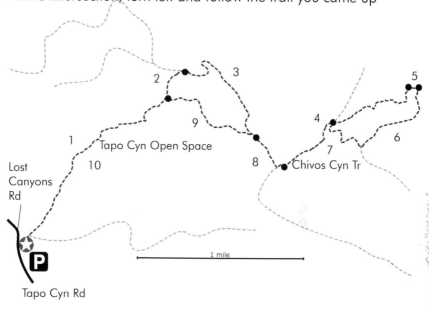

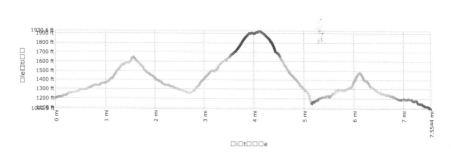

Las Llajas Canyon Trail to Rocky Peak Trail 🚴 🧗 🏇

Highlights:	Scenic, partially shady, moderate wide fire road along the canyon floor with a climb to Rocky Peak Fire Rd to Devils Cyn junction
Miles:	5.2 miles one way; 10.4 miles round trip
Elevation:	1600 ft
Estimated time:	biking: 1-2 hrs hiking and horseback riding: 3-4 hrs
Technical:	★★ ☆ ☆ ☆
Aerobic:	★★★ ☆ ☆
Restrooms:	no
Water:	no
Dogs:	on leash
Parking:	Evening Sky Drive is free

Directions to Trailhead: GPS 34.297009,-118.680298
Evening Sky Drive, Simi Valley
118 Fwy: exit 29 Yosemite Ave .3 mile. North on Yosemite Ave 1.3 miles. Right on Evening Sky Dr .5 mile. Las Llajas trail is on the left.
*Elevation and mileage are approximate.

Overview: Elevation includes out and back. There is partial shade on this trail. Las Llajas Cyn Tr is a wide trail of moderate grade, soft smooth footing with sandy sections. This route is good for equestrians, novice mountain bikers, and families. Some trail users turn around just before the climb at the oil well. After passing the oil well, the trail climbs quickly to Rocky Peak Fire Rd descending to Devils Cyn junction. Street parking is available on Evening Sky Drive in a residential neighborhood. There is dirt on the side of the road next to the trailhead adequate for a horse trailer with room to stand the horse on the side of the street. **(1)** As you begin the trail on the west side of the street, the trail descends down an asphalt path behind houses on Evening Sky Drive. **(2)** Stay to the right at the split. The asphalt turns into a dirt road after .2 miles and continues along the valley floor 3.2 miles north. The trail is shaded by oak trees and a couple of seasonal water crossings. The trail is well-maintained, wide with firm smooth ground and a couple of sand and rocky sections. **(3)** Just before the trail ends at private property, turn right .2 mile leading to the oil well becoming a gravel road. **(4)** Left at the

Sunrise on Las Llajas Cyn Tr past the oil well

Las Llajas Canyon Trail to Rocky Peak Trail

oil well climbing up hill 1 mile. The grassy hillsides are spotted with oak trees along the wide, steep trail with rewarding views at the top. **(5)** Left at the first junction on Rocky Peak Fire Rd north .8 mile. The next post you come to on the right at an intersection is Devils Cyn. This trail has not been maintained and is overgrown with poison oak. This is a good place to turn around.

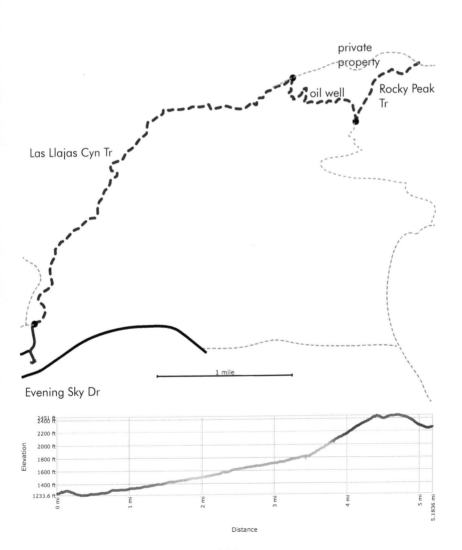

Rocky Peak Trail to Hummingbird Trail

Highlights:	Climb Rocky Peak Fire Rd; descend down Hummingbird, a technical trail with sandstone peaks, drops, slick rock, switchbacks; views
Miles:	6.5 miles
Elevation:	1400 ft
Estimated time:	biking: 1-2 hrs hiking and horseback riding: 2-3 hrs
Technical:	★★★★✦
Aerobic:	★★★☆☆
Restrooms:	no
Water:	no
Dogs:	on leash
Parking:	parking is free

Directions to Trailhead: GPS 34.281993,-118.660173
Hummingbird Trailhead, Keuhner Dr, Simi Valley
23 Fwy: exit 30 for Kuehner Dr. North on Kuehner .1 mile. Park on the dirt lot.
*Elevation and mileage are approximate.

Overview: Horses are allowed, but not recommended on this route. Hummingbird Tr is a popular technical trail with many downhill mountain bikers. Hummingbird is as close to Moab, Utah, as you can get in So Cal. This route begins at the bottom of Hummingbird Tr on Keuhner Dr. You will be ending here. The preferred direction of travel on Hummingbird is downhill. Hikers should do a one way traveling up Hummingbird and returning the same way. Some mountain bikers do the same, although biking up Hummingbird can be very strenuous. To do the loop, there is 3.4 miles on the road leading to Rocky Peak Trailhead leading to Hummingbird Tr. The trailhead is .1 mile north on Keuhner from the parking. **(1)** Follow Keuhner Dr 1.6 miles. The road turns into Santa Susana Pass Rd 1.8 miles gradually climbing up the canyon leading to Rocky Peak. **(2)** Left over the freeway overpass. **(3)** Continue on Rocky Peak Fire Rd .9 mile. The fire road is steep and rocky with panoramic views. There is a trail sign and a bench for Hummingbird Tr. The trail is on the left side. **(4)** Travel down Hummingbird Tr 2.2 miles and meander through caves, drop down sandstone peaks, traverse along the switch backs.

Hummingbird Tr

Rocky Peak Trail to Hummingbird Trail

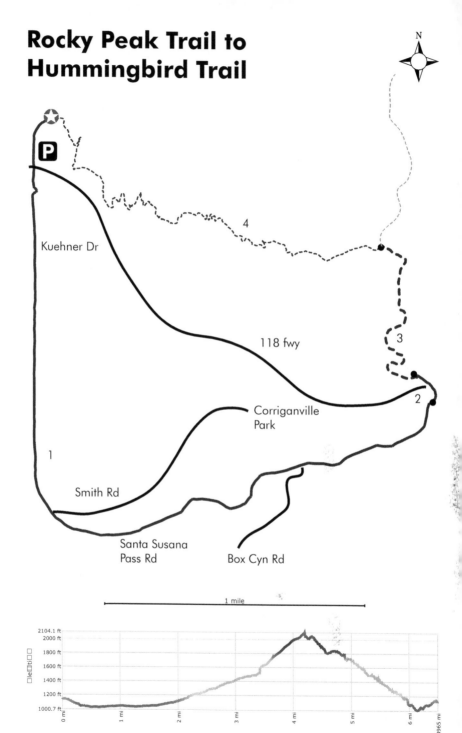

N

P

Kuehner Dr

4

118 fwy

3

2

Corriganville
Park

1

Smith Rd

Santa Susana
Pass Rd

Box Cyn Rd

1 mile

2104.1 ft
2000 ft
1800 ft
1600 ft
1400 ft
1200 ft
1000.7 ft

0 mi   1 mi   2 mi   3 mi   4 mi   5 mi   6 mi   6.4965 mi

Johnson Motorway to Rocky Peak Fire Road Loop

Highlights: Scenic, technical single track climbing up and down sandstone rocks

Miles: 8.3 miles

Elevation: 1850 ft

Estimated time: biking: 1-2 hrs
hiking and horseback riding: 4 hrs

Technical: ★★★★☆

Aerobic: ★★★⯪☆

Restrooms: no

Water: no

Dogs: on leash

Parking: street parking is free

Directions to Trailhead: GPS 34.277527,-118.616762

Iverson Rd, Chatsworth

118 Fwy: exit 32 for Rocky Peak. East on Santa Susana Pass Rd 1.3 miles. Left on Iverson Rd .4 mile. Park on Iverson Rd at the fwy underpass outside the gate.

*Elevation and mileage are approximate.

Overview: The footing is sandstone rocks with sandy sections. The hills are moderate with a couple of steep technical sections. Horses are allowed on the trails, although there is public access granted through the private community limited to trail use for pedestrians and cyclists, restricting access for equestrians. There are approximately 2 miles of street riding on Santa Susana Pass Rd down the hill. The trail begins through a private community. Please do not wander around the community. Follow the signs along the DG path on the side of the street leading to the main trail. The footing is mainly sandstone, some dirt, and sections of sand. The grade is moderate with a few short, steep, rocky sections. The trail is very scenic surrounded by sandstone peaks and coastal sage scrub. There is no shade the entire ride. **(1)** The loop begins up Iverson Rd turning into Johnson Mtwy northwest 3.3 miles up a technical single track with a 1300 ft elevation gain. **(2)** Left on Rocky Peak Fire Rd 3.2 miles. **(3)** Cross the freeway; left on Santa Susana Pass Rd 1.7 miles, **(4)** Left on Iverson Rd .1 mile.

Johnson Mtwy

Johnson Motorway to
Rocky Peak Fire Road Loop

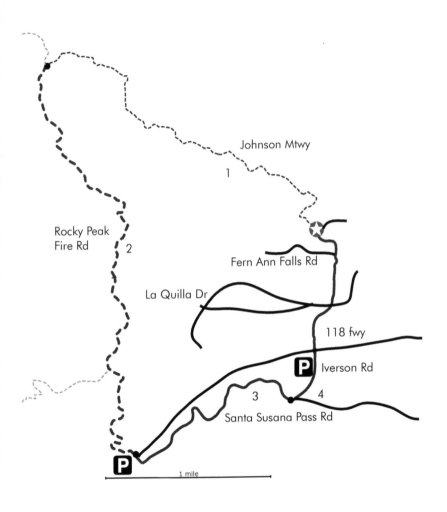

Johnson Mtwy

1

Rocky Peak
Fire Rd

2

Fern Ann Falls Rd

La Quilla Dr

118 fwy

P Iverson Rd

3   4

Santa Susana Pass Rd

P

1 mile

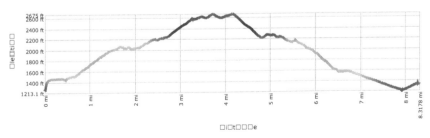

Johnson Motorway to Chumash Trail

Highlights:	Scenic, technical single track climbing up and down sandstone rocks
Miles:	6.4 miles one-way
Elevation:	1450 ft
Estimated time:	biking: 1-2 hrs.
	hiking and horseback riding: 4 hrs
Technical:	★★★★☆
Aerobic:	★★★☆☆
Restrooms:	no
Water:	no
Dogs:	on leash
Parking:	street parking is free

Directions to Trailhead: GPS 34.277527,-118.616762
Iverson Rd, Chatsworth
118 Fwy: exit 32 for Rocky Peak. East on Santa Susana Pass Rd. 1.3 miles. Left on Iverson .4 mile. Park on Iverson Rd at the fwy underpass outside the gate.
*Elevation and mileage are approximate.

Overview: There are approximately 4 miles of street riding to connect the trails. The trail begins through a private community. Public access trail use is granted for pedestrians and cyclists, restricting access for equestrians. (Equestrians can do an out-and-back reverse ride take the Chumash Tr to Johnson Mtwy beginning at the end of Flannagan Dr off of Yosemite Ave.) The footing is mainly rocky with sandstone, some dirt, and sections of sand. The grade is moderate with a few short steep rocky sections. The trail is very scenic surrounded by sandstone peaks and coastal sage scrub. There is full sun the entire ride. **(1)** The loop begins up Iverson Rd follow the signs along the DG path on the side of the street leading to the main trail turning into Johnson Mtwy northwest 3.3 miles up a technical single track with a 1300 ft elevation gain. **(2)** Right on Rocky Peak Fire Rd .5 mile along the ridge. **(3)** Left on Chumash Tr 2.6 miles down a technical rocky trail. The trail rolls over sandstones, skirts along the edge with a drop on one side. The trail comes out at Flannagan Dr. Equestrians should use caution climbing over the boulders and around the tight turns with drops on one side.

Chumash Tr

Johnson Motorway to Chumash Trail

Mountain bikers travel down these trails at a fast speed.

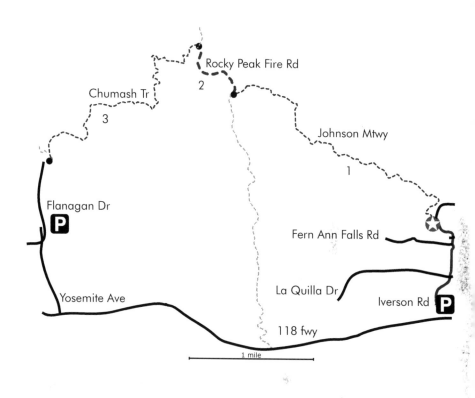

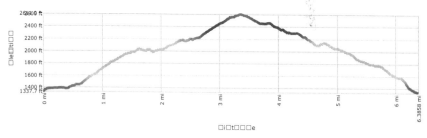

Runkle Canyon Open Space

Rancho Simi Park and Recreation

Located in the Simi Hills on the south side of the 118 Freeway with approximately 1,400 acres of open space. A large parking lot at the public equestrian center is located in Simi Hills on a nine-acre lot. The facilities include a restroom, drinking fountain, picnic bench, an arena, horse trough next to a hitching post and ample equestrian and automobile parking in the shady parking lot. Hours of operation are 6 am to sunset. When exiting the park for a trail ride, there is a gate toward the northwest end of the equestrian center that has a chain that is looped, but not locked. The workmen have asked for the gate to be closed and the chain looped upon exiting. This area gets warm in the summer with full sun exposure.

Albertson Mtwy looking down on Runkle Hill

Simi Equestrian Center to Rim of the Valley Trail

Highlights:	Very remote; a quiet arena with direct trail access to Rim of the Valley Tr
Miles:	3.4 miles loop
Elevation:	700 ft
Estimated time:	biking: 45-1 hr
	hiking and horseback riding: 1-1.5 hrs
Technical:	★★★☆☆
Aerobic:	★★★☆☆
Restrooms:	yes
Water:	drinking fountain
Dogs:	on leash
Parking:	parking lot is free

Directions to Trailhead: GPS 34.262767,-118.728143
3495 Chicory Leaf Place, Simi Valley
23 Fwy: exit 25 Sycamore Dr .3 mile. Right on Sycamore Dr .1 mile. Left on Cochran St .8 mile. Right on Sequoia Ave .6 mile. Left onto Chicory Leaf Pl. Destination is at the end of the street.
*Elevation and mileage are approximate.

Overview: The trail begins at the Arroyo Simi Equestrian Center at the north end of the parking lot. The footing is firm smooth ground, and patches of sand with rocks. The grade is moderate to steep. **(1)** Follow the trail east (right turn) that follows next to the fence line along the parking area. The trail descends down a small hill leading to the wash .4 mile. **(2)** Make a right at the second right uphill for approximately 300 ft. The footing is uneven and partially rutted. **(3)** At the junction follow the Runkle Fire Rd. to the right for 1.1 miles. The trail will ascend and descend close to the neighborhood and quickly climbs back up the hill away from houses. At the next junction, make a left .3 mile. This section of the trail is very picturesque with open fields in the distance. **(4)** At the next junction turn left .4 mile. **(5)** Go around the gate and stay on the trail to the left down the hill .8 mile. You should be at the intersection where you started. **(6)** Make a right for approximately 300 ft down the steep rutted trail. **(7)** Left on the wash .4 mile. **(8)** Take the second trail on the left going uphill. Walk along the outside of the parking lot and back to the gate.

Simi Equestrian Center to Rim of the Valley Trail

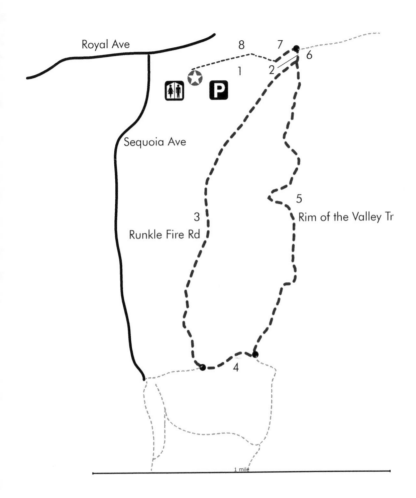

Royal Ave

8

7

1

2

6

Sequoia Ave

5

Rim of the Valley Tr

3

Runkle Fire Rd

4

1 mile

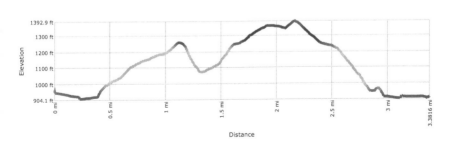

Sage Ranch

Santa Monica Mountains Conservancy

Sage Ranch is located in the Simi Hills nestled on the northwestern plateau of Simi Valley at the LA–Ventura County Line. The park includes 625 acres with a 2.4 mile loop of massive sandstone rock outcroppings, and panoramic views. The trails are lined with coastal sage scrub, chaparral, and native grasses. The park offers an ampitheatre, picnic tables, ten camping sites, restrooms, and a drinking fountain. There are two parking lots. The lower lot is free, and the upper parking lot is $5 and has room to accommodate a truck and trailer. The lower parking lot is narrow with little room to park a trailer.

Camping reservations: 818-999-3753

Sage Ranch Loop

Highlights:	This loop travels along a plateau among sandstone rock formations and coastal sage scrub; with panoramic views
Miles:	2.4 miles
Elevation:	400 ft
Estimated time:	biking: 20-30 mins
	hiking and horseback riding: 40 mins-1 hr.
Technical:	★★ ☆ ☆ ☆
Aerobic:	★★ ☆ ☆ ☆
Restrooms:	porta potty
Water:	drinking fountain
Dogs:	on leash
Parking:	parking lot: $5 main parking lot; free at small lower parking lot

Directions to Trailhead: GPS 34.241626,-118.675529
1 Black Canyon Road, Simi Valley
101 Fwy: exit Valley Circle/Mulholland north 6 miles to Woolsey Cyn Rd. Left to Black Cyn Rd and turn right. The entrance is on the left.
*Elevation and mileage are approximate.

Overview: This trail is a great getaway in a beautiful remote area with mountain views. There is no shade on this loop. The

Sage Ranch Tr

Sage Ranch Loop

footing is firm and smooth with sandy patches. The hills are moderate. The entire loop seems downhill with a coupleshort uphills in the counterclockwise direction. This makes a good short hike, horseback ride, and mountain bike ride. You can begin from either of the parking lots. **(1)** If you parked at the lower lot, head uphill to the left towards the bigger lot .3 mile. **(2)** There is a trailhead to the right next to the restrooms. Follow the trail 2.1 miles in a counterclockwise loop. The scenery is lovely surrounded by sandstone peaks and coastal sage scrub for most of the trip. Follow the trail signs; the loop will end at the lower parking lot.

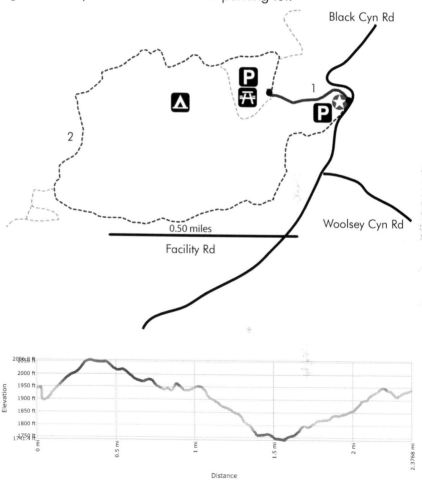

Wood Ranch/Woodridge/ Challenger Park

Rancho Simi Recreation and Park District
Santa Monica Mountains Conservancy

Located at the southern end of Simi Valley, the area offers miles of trails connecting to lang Ranch and other adjoining open space areas. The footing is smooth and scenery is spectacular with the extensive oak woodlands, chaparral, and coastal sage scrub lining the trails. The terrain varies greatly from rolling hills to steep hills. This is a great place to explore for mountain biking, hiking, and horseback riding. There are lights at the signals with a push button for pedestrians, and a raised button for equestrians. Fences run along the streets with dirt paths. Coyote Park public arena is equipped with a drinking fountain, benches, and automatic horse waterer, and hitching posts. There are two main parking lots to access the trails. The Challenger Park parking lot is located at the east end of Long Canyon Rd, which provides quick access to Oak Cyn Tr and Montgomery Tr. The parking lot is set back from the street equipped witht hitching posts in the shde and trash cans. There is enough room to park many horse trailers with a turn around at the end of the parking lot. Adjacent to Challenger Park is a private community called Bridle Trails. Long Cyn parking lot is located at the west side of Long Cyn Rd at the Long Cyn trailhead. The parking lot gets full quickly on weekends. There is no available restrooms or drinking fountains.

Woodridge Loop Tr

Wood Ranch Canyon Loop

Highlights:	Non-technical, pleasant trail climbs up and down the canyon in partial shade; family trail
Miles:	4.9 miles
Elevation:	700 ft
Estimated time:	biking: 45 mins:1 hr.
	hiking & horseback riding: 1-1.5 hrs
Technical:	★★☆☆☆
Aerobic:	★★★☆☆
Restrooms:	no
Water:	no
Dogs:	on leash
Parking:	parking lot is free

Directions to Trailhead: GPS 34.240615,-118.778386
Challenger Park, 298 First St, Simi Valley
23 Fwy: exit 17 Olsen Rd east .3 mile. Right on Olsen Rd 1.9 miles. Right on Wood Ranch Pkwy 1.9 miles. Left on Long Canyon Rd/ Wood Ranch Pkwy 1.7 miles. Right onto Challenger Park. Bluegrass St is on the left. Destination on the right.
118 Fwy south: exit 23 for First St. Left on First St 2.8 miles. Left into Challenger Park.
*Elevation and mileage are approximate.

Overview: Most of the trail is exposed to the sun with little shade. This scenic trail is good for novice mountain bikers, hikers, and equestrians. The footing is firm and smooth. They came be loose due to horse traffic. The hills are moderate with a couple steep sections. **(1)** The trail begins at the back of Challenger Park parking lot. Do not cross the street. Follow the trail uphill as it bends to left .4 mile. **(2)** At the second intersection turn right .75 mile surrounded by coastal sage scrub and chaparral. **(3)** Left on Montgomery Tr 2.1 miles meandering along grassy hillsides leading to a gradual climb offering rewarding views. As the trail descends, the trail narrows and winds down the canyon. **(4)** At bottom of hill, right turn on Oak Canyon Tr .75 mile traveling north along a moderately shaded, wide trail along riparian woodlands. **(5)** At the intersection near the street, turn right up a small hill .1 mile to the split. **(6)** Continue straight .75 mile gradually merging to the left the way you came. **(7)** At the second intersection with a big hill in sight and picnic tables to the right take the trail to the left .4 mile. (You will have passed two small hills.) **(8)** Right at

Long Cyn

Wood Ranch Canyon Loop

the intersection to the parking lot. The parking lot should be seen immediately.

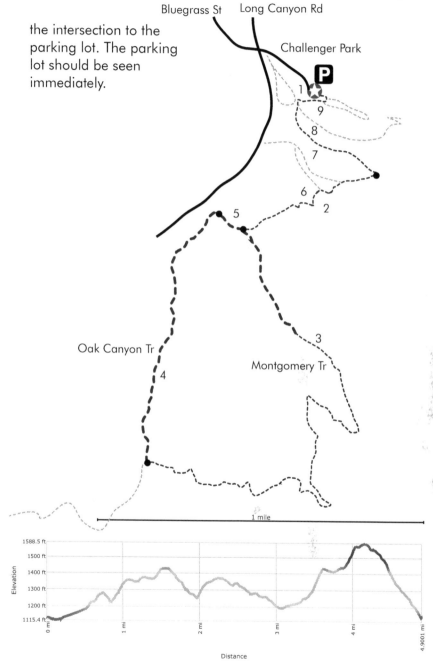

Long Canyon Loop

Highlights:	This loop covers a variety of terrain with a lot of climbing and beautiful views
Miles:	7.75 miles
Elevation:	1600 ft
Estimated time:	biking: 1.5-2 hrs
	hiking and horseback riding: 3-3.5 hrs
Technical:	★★★☆☆
Aerobic:	★★★⯪☆
Restrooms:	no
Water:	no
Dogs:	on leash
Parking:	parking lot is free

Directions to Trailhead: GPS 34.240615,-118.778386
Challenger Park, 298 First St, Simi Valley
23 Fwy north: exit 17 Olsen Rd east .3 mile. Right on Olsen Rd 1.9 miles. Right on Wood Ranch Pkwy 1.9 miles. Left on Long Canyon Rd/Wood Ranch Pkwy 1.7 miles. Right onto Challenger Park. Bluegrass St is on the left. Destination on the right.
118 Fwy south: exit 23 for First St. Left on First St 2.8 miles. Left into Challenger Park.
*Elevation and mileage are approximate.
There is a turn around at the end of the parking lot.

Long Cyn

Long Canyon Loop

Overview: There is a lot of climbing on this ride. You will cross the street twice with a crosswalk signal. The footing is firm smooth ground, but soft in places. The grade is moderate with a couple steep hills. **(1)** The trail begins at the Challenger Park trailhead with a short steep hill from Challenger Park .1 mile. **(2)** At the first junction turn left .4 mile with a gradual climb. **(3)** Take the second right turn that drops down a small hill and immediately climbs up a short hill .7 mile. **(4)** Left at the next junction on Montgomery Canyon Tr 1.4 miles. Montgomery Canyon Tr takes you through a grassy meadow with a gradual grade. The trail becomes steeper as you near the top of the hill with panoramic views. **(5)** Beginning the descent, the trail narrows down the canyon on a lovely trail with gradual turns surrounded by coastal sage scrub .7 mile. **(6)** The trail comes to a junction at Oak Canyon Trail. Left turn (south) up the hill leading to Lang Ranch .6 mile. **(7)** Left at the fire road .2 mile. **(8)** Right at the next junction on Sunrise Tr .2 mile. This section of the trail you will be riding along a ridgeline rocky trail surrounded by sandstone peaks. **(9)** Right on Long Canyon trail for .7 mile which will lead you down the hill to Long Canyon Rd on a steep single track trail with some rocks. **(10)** When you are at the Long Canyon parking lot, stay on the DG path along the fence which continues to the right on Long Canyon Rd. **(11)** Cross Wood Ranch Pkwy at the crosswalk signal and continue the trail on the other side of the street. **(12)** Traveling up Canyon View Tr with houses on both sides, the trail rolls along the ridgeline with panoramic views for .8 mile. **(13)** Almost at the top of the very steep hill, the Wood Ranch Tr intersects to the left with a fairly steep grade .4 mile descending down the hill leading to Coyote Tr. **(14)** Coyote Tr. has a gradual grade with sweeping turns in and out of the trees .7 mile. The trail leads to the an arena and park. **(15)** Right turn at the park .7 mile; ride through the sandy trail leading to Wood Canyon Rd. **(16)** Left turn at the intersection for 200 ft. Cross the street at the crosswalk signal. **(17)** Follow the trail to the right leading up the hill and continue straight down to the Challenger parking lot .1 mile.

Long Canyon Loop

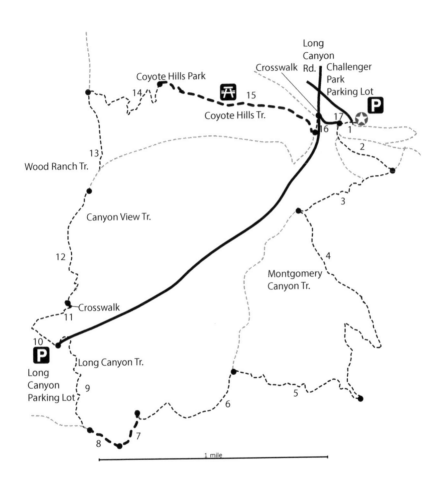

Coyote Hills Park

Coyote Hills Tr.

14

15

Long
Canyon
Rd.

Crosswalk

Challenger
Park
Parking Lot

17

16

1

2

13

Wood Ranch Tr.

Canyon View Tr.

3

12

4

Montgomery
Canyon Tr.

Crosswalk

11

10

Long Canyon Tr.

Long
Canyon
Parking Lot

9

6

5

7

8

1 mile

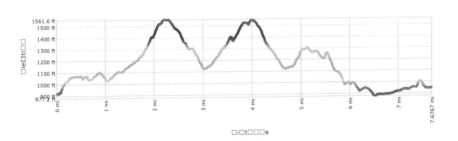

Long Canyon to Woodridge Trail

Highlights:	Steep and rocky trail with views of the Bard Reservoir and surrounding mountains
Miles:	5 miles
Elevation:	900 ft
Estimated time:	biking: 45 mins-1 hr
	hiking and horseback riding: 1-2 hrs
Technical:	★★★☆☆
Aerobic:	★★★☆☆
Restrooms:	no
Water:	no
Dogs:	on leash
Parking:	Long Cyn parking lot is free

Directions to Trailhead: GPS 34.228268,-118.803352
Long Canyon parking lot, Long Canyon Rd, Simi Valley
23 Fwy north: exit 17 Olsen Rd .3 mile. Right on Olsen Rd 1.9 miles. Right on Wood Ranch Pkwy 1.9 mile. It is on the corner of Long Canyon Rd and Wood Ranch Pkwy.
118 Fwy south: exit 23 First St. Left on First St 4.5 miles. It is on the corner of Long Canyon Rd and Wood Ranch Pkwy.
*Elevation and mileage are approximate.

Long Cyn

Long Canyon to Woodridge Trail

Overview: There is a lot of climbing. The footing is firm, uneven and rocky in places. The hills are moderate to steep. The entrance from the Long Cyn parking lot to the trail is a little tricky. Head towards the entrance of the parking lot. Left on Bannister Way for approximately 50 ft. Take the trail on the left. You will cross over a large drainage ditch twice. Equestrians can do a reverse ride out and back to avoid the ditches beginning up Long Cyn Tr. **(1)** Head south .9 mile along a moderate grade trail with wonderful sandstone peaks **(2)** Right at the junction and continue across the street and back on the trail 1.2 miles on the Woodridge Loop Tr. Stay straight at the junction. **(3)** The trail comes out on Sunset Hills Blvd. Cross Sunset Hills Blvd and go through the parking lot for 50 ft to the stepover on the left. Continue up the trail 1.2 miles through a meadow and in between houses. The trail crosses a street and continues directly across the street continuing on an asphalt road along a stream bed shaded with beautiful sycamore trees. **(4)** You are soon on dirt again. When the trail splits, stay to the right .2 mile. **(5)** Left at the next junction on the Sunrise Tr. .9 mile up the steep, rocky trail with reservoir views **(6)** Left on Long Cyn Tr down the steep switchbacks .7 mile to the parking lot.

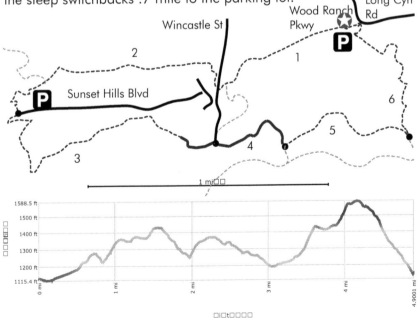

Hillcrest Open Space

Conejo Open Space Conservation Agency

Hillcrest Open Space is located in central Thousand Oaks in between Hillcrest Dr, Avenida De Los Arboles, Erbes Rd, and Westlake Blvd. The area is very wide open with no shade and mainly fireroads. Sage is abundant in the area as well as walnut trees spotting the hillsides. This area is great for training with non-technical wide steep hills and firm footing. There are two main trails to this loop: White Sage Trail with a gradual grade, leads to Hillcrest Ridge Trail, offering 360 degree views and a much steeper grade. There are trailheads on Hillcrest Dr, Westlake Blvd, La Granada Dr, and Conejo School Rd. Street parking is available on Conejo School Rd and La Granada Dr. Trailer parking is recommended on the corner of La Granada Dr and Crown View Ct. The street is wide with plenty of room to turn a trailer around.

View of White Sage Tr in the springtime

Hillcrest Open Space

Highlights: Wide fire roads with panoramic views
Miles: 4.5 miles
Elevation: 1400 ft
Estimated time: biking: 45 mins-1.5 hrs
hiking and horseback riding: 1-2 hrs
Technical: ★★☆☆☆
Aerobic: ★★★½☆
Restrooms: no
Water: no
Dogs: on leash
Parking: street parking on La Granada Dr

Directions to Trailhead: GPS 34.185944,-118.837556
La Granada Dr, Thousand Oaks
23 Fwy: exit 14 for Janss Rd. Right on Janss Rd .7 mile. Right on La Granada Dr .1 mile. The street becomes Crown View Ct.
Park on the corner of Crown View Ct and La Granada Dr.
*Elevation and mileage are approximate.

Overview: The recommended direction of travel for mountain biking and hiking is counter clockwise traveling down the steep hill, and clockwise for horseback riders traveling up the steep hill. This area is wide open with no shade, steep non-technical hills, and wide fire roads. The footing is hard packed with few rocks. There are panoramic views on the ridge. This area is dry with sage shrubs and walnut trees. **(1)** Park near the cul-de-sac on La Granada Dr. Head up the street on Crown View Ct. The trail begins at the end of La Granada Dr .1 mile north on Crown View Ct. There are two other trailheads visible from the parking area. Do not take them. Go up Crown View Ct .1 mile. The trail is just before the first house on the right side of the street. This is the easiest way to connect to the fire road. There isn't a trail sign or a stepover, just a path. **(2)** The single track is .2 mile. Pass behind the house and connect to White Sage Tr. **(3)** Right on the White Sage Tr 1 mile with a gradual grade. The trail will pass many junctions but stay on the main trail. When the trail drops down a hill and climbs back up the hill, it will bend to the left where the trail now becomes Hillcrest Ridge Tr. **(4)** Continue on Hillcrest Ridge Tr. 1.5 miles riding along the ridge with a few steep hills and lovely panoramic views. The trail will come to a junction, overlooking Simi Valley to the north, and houses to the left.

Hillcrest Open Space

(5) Left turn .2 mile. **(6)** Left turn 1.1 miles along a moderate grade. **(7)** Right turn down the single track that you came up on .2 mile. **(8)** Left turn down crown View Ct .1 mile.

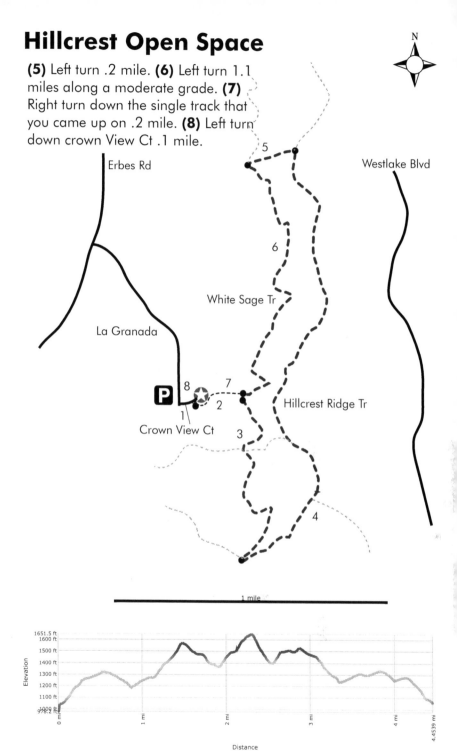

Lang Ranch Open Space

Conejo Open Space Conservation Agency

This beautiful area includes approximately 1,900 acres located in the northeast section of Thousand Oaks. There are over 20 miles of multi-use trails connecting to 8,000 acres of open space including Cheeseboro/Palo Comado Canyons in Agoura and Long Canyon/Challenger Park in Simi Valley. The trails in Lang Ranch and Woodridge are mostly wide, well groomed, moderate grade, few rocks, and open terrain. Some of the trails in Sunset Hills open space connect throughout the community, and some lead down the hill and loop near the Bard Reservoir. They are a little steeper and rockier with panoramic views of the Bard Reservoir and surrounding mountains. The native vegetation, coastal sage scrub, oak woodlands, rock outcroppings, and panoramic views add to the splendor of the area. The trail system is popular among local residents for biking, hiking, and horseback riding. With many trails to choose from, the area doesn't seem to get too crowded.

There are 4 trailhead entrances and three of them are within approximately 1/2 mile of each other and provide direct access to Lang Ranch. Two trailheads are on Lang Ranch Parkway, the trailhead closest to Westlake Blvd joins the Oakbrook Vista Trail leading to Westlake Village. An alternate trailhead is at the end of Lang Ranch Parkway leading to Albertson Motorway. There is a trailhead on the corner of Autumn Ridge Dr/Oak Valley Ln and Westlake Blvd with access to Autumn Ridge Trail, Meadow Vista Trail, and Alapay Trail with connecting trails to Simi Valley. The parking for the trailheads is on the street with a decomposed granite sidewalk connecting the trailheads along the road. There is room to tie a horse on the side of the trailer on the DG path. Please clean up after your horse. People walk on the DG path and there are houses in the vicinity. The dirt parking lot at the end of Sunset Hills Blvd can be utilized for the trails to the reservoir as well as Lang Ranch following the Woodridge Loop Trail to Alapay Trail. This parking lot is rarely used and is adequate for horse trailers. There aren't any restrooms or drinking fountains. This area dries well after a rain.

Meadow Vista Trail/ Alapay Trail

Highlights:	Pleasant trail with panoramic views; family trail
Miles:	4.1 miles
Elevation:	800 ft
Estimated time:	biking: 30 min-1 hr
	hiking and horseback riding: 1-1.5 hrs
Technical:	★★☆☆☆
Aerobic:	★★★☆☆
Restrooms:	no
Water:	no
Dogs:	on leash
Parking:	street parking is free

Directions to Trailhead: GPS 34.212876,-118.810428
Lang Ranch Pkwy, Thousand Oaks
23 Fwy: exit Avenida De Los Arboles. East on Avenida De Los Arboles. Right on Westlake Blvd. Next left on Lang Ranch Pkwy. Trailhead is at the end of the street on the right side.
*Elevation and mileage are approximate.

Overview: This route is good for horseback riding, mountain biking, and hiking. The streets are wide with dirt sidewalks and there is plenty of street parking to accommodate a horse trailer. The footing is firm and smooth for most of the ride with a couple of sections of rocks. You will be in full sun almost the entire time. The trail is wide (approximately 10 ft) for most of the ride except .25 mile through the trees. The trail skirts along the edge of the mountain north. The trailhead begins at the end of Lang Ranch Pkwy. **(1)** Follow Albertson Mtwy 1 mile. Albertson Mtwy begins as a flat wide trail along the valley floor. The first junction you come to is Alapay Tr. You will be returning on Alapay Tr. **(2)** Follow signs for the public trail. Stay to the left at the split to stay on Albertson Mtwy. The trail turns into a single track gradually winding through the oak trees. **(3)** Left turn at the junction on the Meadow Vista Tr up a long gradual climb on a wide open fire road 1.2 miles reaching the top of the hillside where there is a bench awaiting you with panoramic views at the top. **(4)** Descent down the hill .2 mile. **(5)** Left at the next junction up the hill on Alapay Trail .9 mile heading south. The trail skirts the edge of the hill with full sun exposure.

Overlooking Simi Valley on Meadow Vista Tr

(6) Right at the next junction leading to a flat walk along the valley floor back on Albertson Mtwy .4 mile heading back to the trail-head.

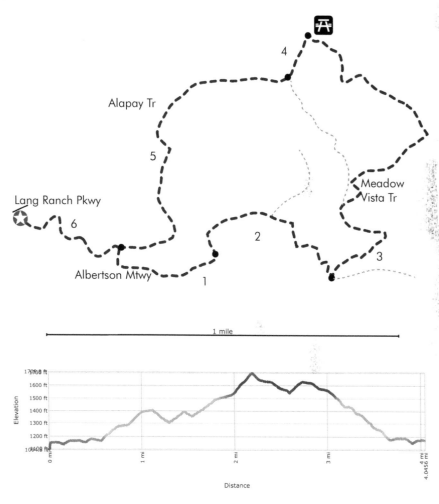

167

Autumn Ridge to Montgomery Trail

Highlights:	Nice getaway; non-technical ride with firm, smooth footing, and nice views
Miles:	7.1 miles
Elevation:	1400 ft
Estimated time:	biking: 1-2 hrs hiking and horseback riding: 2- 2.5 hrs.
Technical:	★★☆☆☆
Aerobic:	★★★½☆
Restrooms:	no
Water:	no
Dogs:	on leash
Parking:	street parking is free

Directions to Trailhead: GPS 34.216447,-118.815781
Oak Valley Ln, Thousand Oaks
23 Fwy: exit Avenida De Los Arboles. East on Avenida De Los Arboles. Left on Westlake Blvd. Right on Oak Valley Ln. Park On Oak Valley Ln. The trail is on the north (left) side of Westlake Blvd.
*Elevation and mileage are approximate.

Overview: This is one of my favorite horseback riding trails in the area. The footing is firm and smooth with soft sections due to horse travel. This route doesn't get crowded on weekends and holidays and is recommended for mountain bikers, horseback riders, and hikers. **(1)** The route begins on Autumn Ridge Tr, a wide open fire road that climbs up a hill with a short steep climb to the right .5 mile. **(2)** The fire road plateaus as the pleasant gradual trail rolls along the grassy hillside contouring the hill .9 mile. The area provides full sun exposure for most of the ride. **(3)** Once you are at the junction at the top of the hill, the trail is approximately 10 ft to the left, if facing Simi Valley, and an immediate right turn on the fire road. Descend down the hill .2 mile north towards Simi Valley. **(4)** Make a right (east) on the single track Oak Canyon Tr which descends at a mild grade .6 mile. **(5)** At the next intersection continue straight through the oak forest .8 mile. This section of the trail is almost flat on a wide trail. Coming out of the oak trees there is full sun exposure for the remainder of the ride. **(6)** Follow the trail to the right 1.4 miles heading northwest through lovely grassy hillsides gradually climbing uphill for a view.

Overlooking Autumn Ridge Tr

Autumn Ridge to Montgomery Tr.

(7) The descent is a single track that winds .7 mile down the canyon to Oak Canyon Tr. **(8)** The trail continues back the way you came. Left turn on Oak Canyon Tr .6 mile. **(9)** At the junction left up the fireroad .2 mile. **(10)** Continue straight (a slight left) then right .9 mile on Autumn Ridge Tr descending to the left at the bottom of the hill.

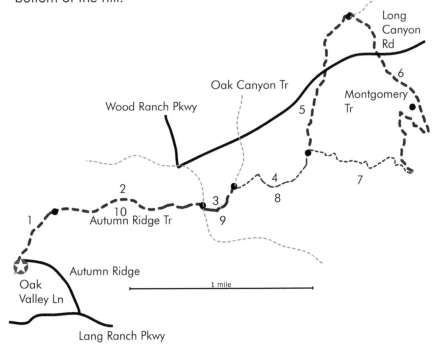

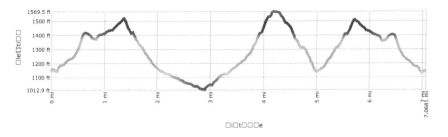

Albertson to China Flat

Highlights:	Well-maintained fire road; long climb; grassy meadow; panoramic views
Miles:	7.75 miles
Elevation:	1400 ft
Estimated time:	biking: 1-2 hrs
	hiking and horseback riding: 2-3 hrs
Technical:	★★ ☆ ☆ ☆
Aerobic:	★★★ ☆
Restrooms:	no
Water:	no
Dogs:	on leash
Parking:	Lang Ranch Pkwy is free

Directions to Trailhead: GPS 34.212876,-118.810428
Lang Ranch Pkwy, Thousand Oaks
23 Fwy: exit Avenida De Los Arboles. East on Avenida De Los Arboles. Right on Westlake Blvd. Left on Lang Ranch Pkwy. The trail is at the end of the street on the right side.
*Elevation and mileage are approximate.

Overview: The Albertson Mtwy provides access from Lang Ranch to Cheeseboro/Palo Comado Canyon and Simi Valley. The fire road is used by mountain bikers, equestrians and hikers. The footing is firm and smooth and the grade is moderate with full sun exposure. This trail doesn't get crowded because usage is limited to strong riders and hikers traveling up the long climb. Mountain bikers travel at a fast speed down the hill. The route begins on Albertson Mtwy on a wide open, well-maintained fireroad with sandstone rock outcroppings and coastal sage scrub along the trail. **(1)** The trail climbs steadily east for 2.9 miles to the Palo Comado Cyn Tr. **(2)** Right at the junction on Palo Comado Cyn Tr .1 mile leading to China Flat. China Flat is a beautiful grassy meadow with coastal sage scrub in the surrounding hills offering 180 degree panoramic views. **(3)** Right turn on the China Flat single track following the edge of the plateau for approximately 1.2 miles. The Bard Reservoir is in view at times. At the junction if you travel .4 mile (right) west up a steep climb you will reach Simi Peak, the highest point in the area. **(4)** Follow the trail to the left .1 mile leading back to the fire road. **(5)** Left turn on Palo Comado Cyn Tr .4 mile. Return back the way you came turning left down Albertson Mtwy.

China Flat Loop Tr

Albertson to China Flat

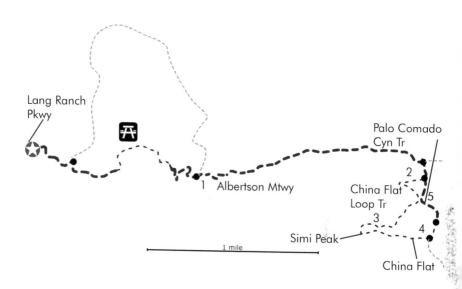

Lang Ranch Pkwy

Albertson Mtwy

1

Palo Comado Cyn Tr

2

5

China Flat Loop Tr

3

Simi Peak

4

China Flat

1 mile

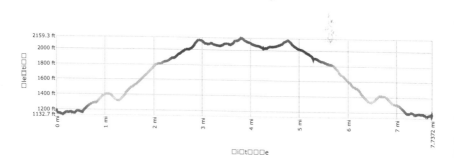

2159.3 ft
2000 ft
1800 ft
1600 ft
1400 ft
1200 ft
1132.7 ft

0 mi   1 mi   2 mi   3 mi   4 mi   5 mi   6 mi   7 mi   7.7372 mi

China Flat (Dead Cow) Loop 🚴 🥾 🐎

Highlights:	Steep, rocky and rutted technical trail; fun single track; long downhill with views
Miles:	10 miles
Elevation:	2100 ft
Estimated time:	biking: 1.5-2.5 hrs hiking and horseback riding: 3-4 hrs
Technical:	★★★★⯪
Aerobic:	★★★★☆
Restrooms:	no
Water:	no
Dogs:	on leash
Parking:	street parking is free

Directions to Trailhead: GPS 34.212876,-118.810428
Lang Ranch Pkwy, Thousand Oaks
23 Fwy: exit Avenida De Los Arboles. East on Avenida De Los Arboles. Right on Westlake Blvd. Next left on Lang Ranch Pkwy .1 mile on the right side across the street from the park and before the Chumash Interpretive Center.
*Elevation and mileaage are approximate.

Overview: Not recommended for horses because there are over two miles of street travel. Hikers may begin at the bottom of China Flat for a one-way trip to the top of China Flat. This ride has technical sections and is not a beginner mountain bike ride. The footing is firm ground, rocky, rutted, climbing up sandstone rocks. The hills are moderate to steep with a technical climb. Begin on Lang Ranch Pkwy on the south side of the street across from the park. The sign for Oakbrook Vista trail is on the fence rail. **(1)** Head east on Oakbrook Vista Tr 1 mile up switchbacks followed by a steep climb with rocks and ruts in the trail. **(2)** When you are almost at the top of the first hill, the trail will split; stay slight left uphill and continue .4 mile. The trail descends down a rocky, sometimes overgrown, single track. Go straight through the next junction. **(3)** The trail drops down a fire road and bends to the right up a hill .4 mile. **(4)** After 100 ft hidden Meadows Tr is the first trail on the right heading southeast .8 mile leading to Falling Star Ave. There isn't a sign, and the entrance to the trail can be overgrown. **(5)** Travel 1.3 miles down Falling Star Ave, Left on Pathfinder Ave, right on Dumaine Ave, left on Lindero Cyn, left on St. James Ct. The trailhead is at the end of St. James Ct.

China Flat Tr aka Dead Cow

Top of China Flat Tr

China Flat (Dead Cow) Loop

(6) The trail up China Flat (Dead Cow) 1.5 miles is a long, steep, technical climb with long sections of boulders and ruts in full sun north leading to China Flat a flat meadow. **(7)** Once you go around the gate, the China Flat Loop begins. There is a maze of trails through the meadow. Palo Comado Fire Rd connects to most of the trails. When the trail splits take the second left, then the first right .2 mile, then left on Palo Comado Fire Rd .6 mile. **(8)** Pass the single track on the left and take the next left (west) down Albertson Mtwy 2.9 miles leading to Lang Ranch Pkwy. **(9)** There are .9 mile of street riding along Lang Ranch Pkwy west along the fence to the trailhead.

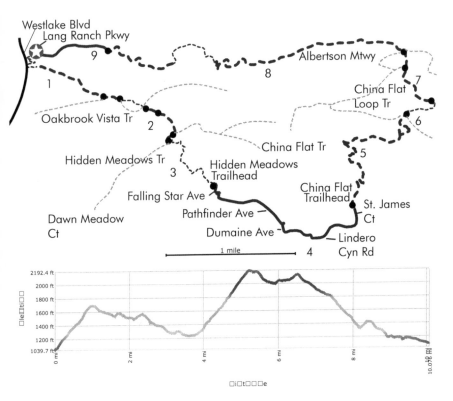

Oakbrook Vista to Sandstone Hills Trail

Highlights:	Remote; sandstone peaks; panoramic views
Miles:	2.9 miles one way
Elevation:	1300 ft
Estimated time:	biking: 1-1.5 hrs
	hiking and horseback riding: 2 hrs
Technical:	★★★◗☆
Aerobic:	★★★★☆
Restrooms:	no
Water:	no
Dogs:	on leash
Parking:	street parking is free

Directions to Trailhead: 34.212876,-118.810428
Lang Ranch Pkwy, Thousand Oaks
23 Fwy: exit Avenida De Los Arboles. East on Avenida De Los Arboles. Right on Westlake Blvd. Next left on Lang Ranch Pkwy .1 mile on the right side across from the park.
*Elevation and mileage are approximate.

Overview: This area is peaceful with nice views with full sun exposure. The trails are mainly wide with moderate to steep hills. Even though this trail is used by hikers and mountain bikers to connect to Oak Park and Westlake Village, it is not crowded; you may only see a couple other trail users. Once the trail passes the connection to Oak Park (on Hidden Meadows Tr), the area becomes remote. There are blind turns on the switchbacks, and a couple areas where you are on the edge of the hill. The footing is firm, smooth ground; rocky, and rutted. The grade is moderate with a couple of steep hills. The route begins on Lang Ranch Pkwy approx .1 mile from Westlake Blvd. The sign for Oakbrook Vista Tr. is on the fence rail. It may be hard to find if a car is blocking it. Keep an eye out for a break in the fence with a stepover. **(1)** This trail begins up Oakbrook Vista, a gentle single track with .3 mile of switchbacks shaded with chaparral and coastal sage scrub leading to a steep rocky, rutted exposed fire road heading east .7 mile. **(2)** Pass through the turn off up a small hill and stay to the left at the split down the hill .4 mile. The trail descends down a rocky, sometimes overgrown single track. Go straight through the next junction. **(3)** The trail drops down a fire road and bends to

Edison Tr

Oakbrook Vista to Sandstone Hills Trail

the right up a hill .3 mile. You will pass a single track on the right. The area from this point on becomes remote. **(4)** Continue straight .5 mile. There are many service roads that are dead ends so stay straight. **(5)** After the top of the steep hill, the trail will split. Stay to the left and continue climbing .7 mile. The trail continues as a fire road surrounded by sandstone boulders leading to Vista Point overlook. The trail dead ends at this point.

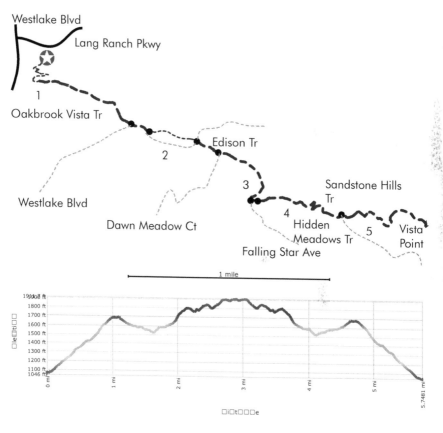

Sunset Hills Trail to Reservoir Loop

Highlights:	Loop near the reservoir with a steep climb; rocky and smooth footing; panoramic views
Miles:	4 miles
Elevation:	875 ft
Estimated time:	biking: 30 mins-1 hr hiking and horseback riding: 1-1.5 hrs
Technical:	★★⯪☆☆
Aerobic:	★★★⯪☆
Restrooms:	no
Water:	no
Dogs:	on leash
Parking:	street parking is free

Directions to Trailhead: GPS 34.22385,-118.82776
Sunset Hills Blvd, Thousand Oaks
23 Fwy: exit Sunset Hills Blvd. East on Sunset Hills Blvd 1 mile. Turn into the dirt parking lot on the right.
*Elevation and mileage are approximate.

Overview: After a rain, the footing can be soft causing holes with horse traffic. This trail has a lot of climbing. If you are looking for seclusion, this trail is rarely traveled. The footing is mainly rocky with smooth footing near the reservoir. The grade is moderate with a long steep climb. The trail begins at the Sunset Hills parking lot. **(1)** Walk along the DG fenced path on Sunset Blvd for approximately 300 ft. Cross the street and continue on the trail .4 miles. The trail is rocky with a few switchbacks. **(2)** At the junction turn left (west) up Sunset Hills Tr and down a long steep hill 1.4 miles. Stay to the left at the split. **(3)** At the next junction turn right .8 mile looping close to the Bard Reservoir. The footing is firm and smooth with rocky sections throughout most of the trail. The freeway noise is heard for a short time when beginning the loop along the newly constructed single track around the reservoir. Once the trail starts to bend around the hill towards the reservoir, the trail becomes surprisingly peaceful. **(4)** Left at the intersection back up the steep hill 1 mile. **(5)** Right at the next intersection down the switchbacks .4 mile to the parking lot.

Loop around the reservoir

Near the freeway around the reservoir

Sunset Hills Trail/Reservoir Loop

N

23 Freeway

Wood Ranch Reservoir

Erbes Rd

3

4

2

Sunset
Hills Tr

1

5

Sunset Hills Blvd

P ☆

1 mile

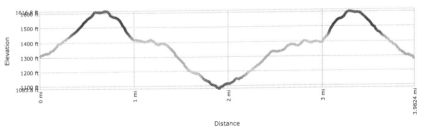

Los Robles Open Space

COSCA
A joint Project of the City of Thousand Oaks and the
Conejo Recreation & Park District
The Santa Monica Mountains Conservancy

Los Robles Open Space includes approximately 2,000 acres of located in the southern section of Conejo Open Space. Los Robles trail connects with the Rancho Sierra Vista/Satwiwa National Park/ Point Mugu State Park. The Los Robles trail bisects other areas of open space from Thousand Oaks to Newbury Park. Approximately 25 miles of multi-use trails are open to the public along the beautiful ridge line trails with many adjoining neighborhood trails winding in narrow canyons through dense chaparral covered slopes, along open grassy meadows, and twist through single track trails. The vast assortment of trails make this area very popular to runners, hikers, mountain bikers, and equestrians. The area has partial shade in the canyons and the oak groves, although the majority of the area receives full sun exposure. The trails dry quickly after a rain.

Several of the trailheads are located at parking lots large enough for cars and horse trailers. In Thousand Oaks the main trailhead at the southern end of Moorpark Rd is a large dirt parking lot. The lot is adequate for horse trailer parking, although the parking lot gets full quickly. One quarter mile on Greenmeadow Dr west of Moorpark Rd there is an asphalt parking area less crowded and adequate for equestrian trailer parking. There are restrooms without running water, a drinking fountain, automatic horse waterer, a dog bowl, a covered bench, and hitching posts. Most trails can be accessed by either trailhead. There is a trailhead at Triunfo Community Park with multiple smaller parking lots, large enough to fit horse trailers. The park can fill up due to activities at the park. There is room to park on the street if needed. There are restrooms and drinking fountains. In Newbury Park the trailhead is on a dirt parking lot on the north side of Potrero Rd, large enough to fit horse trailers and is rarely used. There is a picnic table, drinking fountain, and an automatic horse waterer. This parking lot is behind gates and is open from 9–4. There is off-street parking on Portrero Rd/Wendy Dr. Take the Los Robles Connector Trail that runs along Portrero Rd. to the trailhead.

Spring Canyon Trail

Highlights:	A relaxing neighborhood double track trail with a few small hills, partial views
Miles:	1.6 miles one way; 3.2 miles round trip
Elevation:	300 ft.
Estimated time:	biking: 20-30 mins hiking and horseback riding: 1 hr
Technical:	★★⯪☆☆
Aerobic:	★★☆☆☆
Restrooms:	porta potty
Water:	drinking fountain, dog waterer, automatic horse waterer
Dogs:	on leash
Parking:	Greenmeadow parking lot is free

Directions to Trailhead: GPS 34.17525,-118.885578
Greenmeadow Dr, Thousand Oaks
101 Fwy: exit Moorpark Rd. South on Moorpark Rd .7 mile to the end. Right turn on Greenmeadow .4 mile to the parking area. You can also park at the dirt parking lot on Moorpark Rd.
*Elevation and mileage are approximate.

Overview: This route is an out and back. This is a popular trail used by hikers, families, and mountain bikers. This trail is the connector for the

Los Robles Tr leading to Spring Cyn Tr

Spring Canyon Trail

Los Robles West Tr. The footing is firm with rocks; the grade is moderate. The trail meanders toward Heavenly Valley St in Newbury Park. **(1)** The all-access trail begins on Oak Creek Cyn Tr through an oak grove along a fence separating hikers from horseback riders and bikers .4 mile. Stay right when the trail comes out of the oak trees and is no longer an all-access trail; climbs a short, steep hill. **(2)** Right as the terrain opens up with full sun exposure surrounded by chaparral, coastal sage scrub, and merges with the Los Robles Tr .1 mile. **(3)** Right at the next split 1.1 miles climbing up and over a short rocky hill. Pass Los Robles W. The trail is a moderately flat double track trail with a couple of small hills. It travels alongside houses in the Newbury Park neighborhood leading to an open field and a park. **(4)** Right when the trail comes down a hill and leads to a stepover. There is a path that loops around a field next to a park.

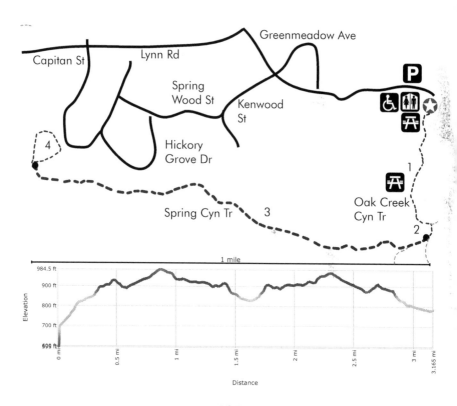

Los Robles to Los Padres Loop

Highlights: Scenic oak groves along a meadow and ascending down switchbacks with narrow bridges

Miles: 4.4 miles

Elevation: 500 ft

Estimated time: biking: 30-45 hrs
hiking and horseback riding: 1.25 hrs

Technical: ★★✦☆☆

Aerobic: ★★✦☆☆

Restrooms: Porta potty

Water: drinking fountain, automatic horse waterer, dog bowl

Dogs: on leash

Parking: parking lot is free

Directions to Trailhead: GPS 34.17525,-118.885578
Greenmeadow Dr, Thousand Oaks
101 Fwy: exit Moorpark Rd. South on Moorpark Rd .7 mile to the end. Right turn on Greenmeadow .4 mile to a parking area.
*Elevation and mileage are approximate.

Overview: There are .3 mile of street travel along a grass strip with trees along the center and the side of Moorpark Rd.

Los Padres Tr

Los Robles to Los Padres Loop

This is one of my favorite local rides for hiking, horseback riding, and mountain biking. These trails can be used as a connector to access other trails. This is a popular trail with hikers and mountain bikers. The footing is firm smooth ground along with a gravel fire road. The hills are moderate with a steep section up the switchbacks near the top of Los Padres Tr. **(1)** Begin through a shaded oak grove on Oak Creek Cyn Loop Tr .4 mile to the first junction. **(2)** Continue right uphill at the junction. Follow signs for Los Robles East Tr .1 mile. **(3)** Stay to the left uphill at the next split .5 mile on a wide trail to the picnic table. **(4)** Right at the picnic table up the well-groomed single track .6 mile. The trail meanders up a gradual hill amongst coastal sage scrub and chapparal leading to a meadow. **(5)** There are two benches overlooking views of the Conejo Valley a couple hundred feet from the junction. Right up the hill passing the benches .5 mile. **(6)** Left at the next junction on the Los Robles Tr approximately .1 mile. **(7)** At the next junction descend down a rocky fire road (left turn) north .5 mile leading to Los Padres Tr. **(8)** Left on Los Padres Tr .6 mile. The trail begins with a few switchbacks, crosses a few narrow wooden bridges, and skirts along the edge of the hillside with soft dirt on the sides of the trail for a short time leading to a beautiful flat riparian woodland oak grove. There are a few low hanging branches that equestrians will need to duck under. **(9)** Coming upon Los Padres Dr, turn left on Los Padres Dr for approximately 300 ft. **(10)** Turn left on Moorpark Rd .3 mile along the grass strip. **(11)** Continue through the dirt parking lot at the end of Moorpark Rd. Go over the stepover heading past the information sign .3 mile. **(12)** When you come to a split, right turn towards Oak Creek Cyn Loop Tr. Turn right .1 mile **(13)** At the split stay to the left to return the way you came .4 mile. Most bikers enjoy the Oak Creek Cyn Loop Tr to the right with many turns and rolling terrain, and hikers and horseback riders enjoy the trail to the left (the way you came) with soft smooth terrain, under oak trees and along the fence.

Los Robles to Los Padres Loop

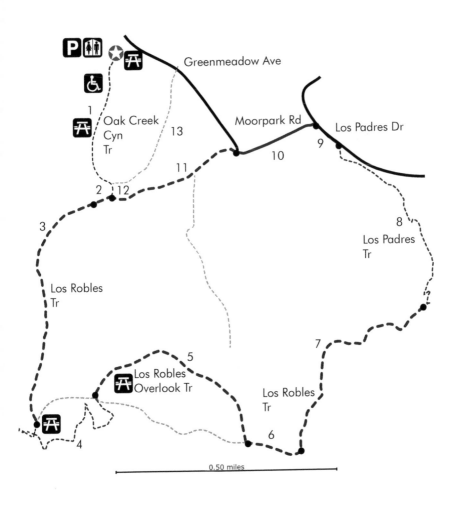

Greenmeadow Ave

Moorpark Rd

Los Padres Dr

1

Oak Creek
Cyn
Tr

13

10

9

11

2 12

3

8
Los Padres
Tr

Los Robles
Tr

7

5

Los Robles
Overlook Tr

Los Robles
Tr

4

6

0.50 miles

188

Los Robles West Trail a.k.a. Space Mountain

Highlights:	Popular single track with switchbacks climbing up and over a picturesque canyon
Miles:	8 miles
Elevation:	1450 ft
Estimated time:	biking: 1.5+hrs hiking and horseback riding: 3+hrs
Technical:	★★★✦☆
Aerobic:	★★★☆☆
Restrooms:	porta potty
Water:	drinking fountain, dog waterer, automatic horse waterer
Dogs:	on leash
Parking:	parking is free

Directions to Trailhead: GPS 34.17525,-118.885578
Greenmeadow Dr, Thousand Oaks
101 Fwy: exit Moorpark Rd. South on Moorpark Rd .7 mile to the end. Right turn on Greenmeadow Dr .4 miles to parking area.
*Elevation and mileage are approximate.

Overview: This trail can also begin at the Moorpark Rd trailhead. This is a favorite for mountain biking. Intermediate riders should be able to ride most, if not all, of this trail, but it is not recommended for beginners. This ride can also be an out and back avoiding street travel or begin at the bottom of Rosewood and hike up to Angel Vista. Equestrians should be cautious on this trail. It is heavily traveled by mountain bikers with many blind turns, drop offs, and 1 mile of street travel. There isn't much shade on the trail, although there are chaparral and coastal sage scrub lining the trail. This loop begins at the Greenmeadow trailhead. **(1)** Take Oak Creek Cyn Loop Tr past the restrooms .4 mile through the oak trees. **(2)** Right turn at the intersection .1 mile. **(3)** Right at the next split uphill and drop down the hill. **(4)** Left at the first intersection on the Los Robles West Tr 2.5 miles. The Los Robles Tr heads west toward Newbury Park with a moderate climb. The trail rolls above the neighborhoods along the edge of a ridgeline, climbs up switchbacks, and has many rocks to maneuver around. You will see private property signs and a small gate. Go through the gate and cross the dirt street to continue on

Angel Vista overlooking Conejo Valley

Angel Vista overlooking Point Mugu

Los Robles West Trail

the trail. Please do not trespass. **(5)** Continue .5 mile up the hill past the next two junctions. There are picnic benches awaiting you at Angel Vista offering rewarding ocean, mountain, and city views. **(6)** Heading down the hill, left at first junction on Rosewood Tr 1.8 miles. This trail is a lot of fun. It is easy to go fast down the switchbacks so please watch your speed, as this is a popular trail. The Rosewood Tr can become slippery for hikers; therefore, it is recommended to bring walking sticks. **(7)** Right on Lynn Rd. Right on Heavenly Valley Rd. Left on Hemlock Ln 50 ft. **(8)** Cross the stepover on Spring Cyn Tr 1 mile. You'll pass Los Robles W junction. **(9)** Up the hill to the next junction and down the hill .1 mile. **(10)** Left at the bottom of the hill .1 mile. **(11)** Left on Oak Creek Cyn Loop Tr. At the split stay to the right .4 mile down the last set of sweeping turns. **(12)** Left on Greenmeadow Ave .1 mile to the car.

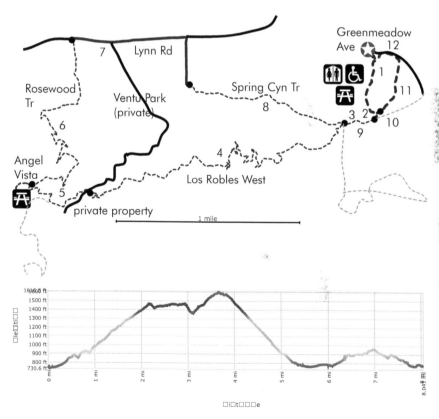

Los Robles East to White Horse Canyon Trail

Highlights:	Single track and fire road with loose rocky sections and steep hills
Miles:	7 miles
Elevation:	1250 ft
Estimated time:	biking: 1-1.5 hrs hiking and horseback riding: 2-3 hrs
Technical:	★★★★☆
Aerobic:	★★★★☆
Restrooms:	Greenmeadow parking lot .4 miles away
Water:	Greenmeadow offers drinking fountain, automatic horse waterer, dog bowl
Dogs:	on leash
Parking:	dirt parking lot is free

Directions to Trailhead: GPS 34.171938,-118.881222
Moorpark Rd, Thousand Oaks
101 Fwy: exit Moorpark Rd. South on Moorpark Rd .7 mile to the end. Park at the dirt parking lot at the end of Moorpark Rd.
*Elevation and mileage are approximate.

Overview: This route has a lot of climbing. The footing on White Horse Tr and Los Robles Tr is rocky and the hills are steep. Los Robles Tr has a moderate grade with mostly smooth footing. This loop can also be accessed from the Greenmeadow parking lot. **(1)** Begin at the Los Robles parking lot at the end of Moorpark Rd. Ride

Los Robles Tr

Los Robles East to White Horse Canyon Trail

down the street on Moorpark Rd .3 mile north along the grass strip the way you drove up. **(2)** Right turn on Los Padres Dr approx. 300 ft; trailhead is on the right. Follow the Los Padres single track .6 mile through the oak grove, across the narrow bridges, and up the switchbacks. Equestrians will need to duck under low branches. The trail skirts along the edge of the hillside with soft dirt on the sides of the trail. **(3)** Right turn (south) up the gravel fire road .5 mile. **(4)** At the junction, left turn on Los Robles Fire Rd for approximately .9 mile. The trail is next to private property surrounded by a barbed wire fence. Please do not trespass. **(5)** After the rocky descent, right turn on the White Horse Tr. This trail also abuts private property. White Horse Tr begins down a steep, loose, and rocky descent. It is a challenging trail for mountain bikers with loose rocks and steep hills. This trail is not for the novice rider. White Horse Tr. makes a loop up and down a few steep hills .7 mile. **(6)** The trail comes upon a very steep hill. There is a single track to the right just before the steep hill. Follow the single track .3 mile. At the top of the hill, you come to an overlook at a junction on Los Robles Tr. There are lovely views at this point. There are old signs "Equestrian trail and Conejo Crest Tr." **(7)** Turn left with a couple steep rocky hills. When the trail splits stay to the right after .4 mile. **(8)** There is a single track on the left .2 mile just before the trail comes upon a very steep, long, rocky hill. **(9)** You are back on White Horse Tr for approximately 200 ft. You should be close to the beginning of White Horse Tr. **(10)** There is a single track to the right .1 mile (sometimes overgrown) leading to the Los Robles Fire Rd. that bypasses the steep, rocky hill you came down. **(11)** Left on the fire road. This is the fire road you came on. The trail will pass a few junctions; stay straight. After 1 mile, you will come to the Los Padres junction. Pass the Los Padres Fire Rd and continue along a lovely, flat meadow .5 mile. Follow signs for the Juan Bautista De Anza Tr. **(12)** When you come to a junction with benches uphill to the right and a steep downhill in front of you, turn left down the gradual partially shaded single track .6 miles. **(13)** The trail comes to a junction with a bench under a shaded tree to the right, left turn to continue down the hill .5 mile. **(14)** Stay straight. The trail will veer slightly to the right passing the next couple junctions .4 mile. The stepover is near the information kiosk.

Los Robles East to White Horse Canyon Trail

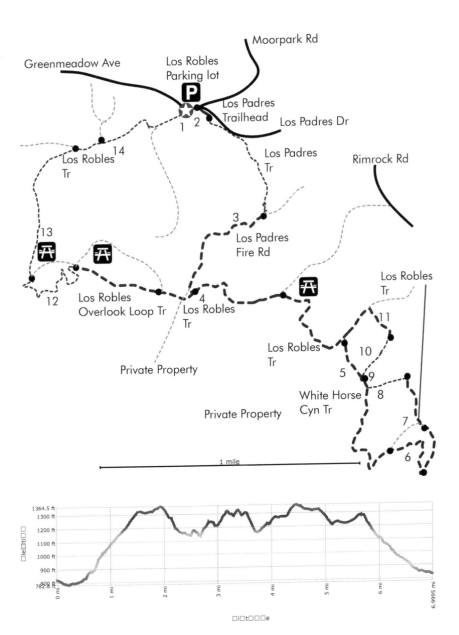

Potrero Road to Angel Vista

Highlights: Scenic single track along a neigborhood; climbs up steep rocky hills to Angel Vista

Miles: 2.5 miles one way; 5 miles round trip

Elevation: 1350 ft

Estimated time: biking: 1 hr

hiking and horseback riding: 2 hrs

Technical: ★★★✦☆

Aerobic: ★★★✦☆

Restrooms: no

Water: drinking fountain, dog waterer, automatic horse waterer

Dogs: on leash

Parking: Potrero Rd parking lot is free

Directions to Trailhead: GPS 34.155426,-118.941894

Potrero Rd, Newbury Park

101 Fwy: exit Wendy Dr. Head south toward the ocean. Left on Portrero Rd .5 mile. The parking lot is on the left side of the street. There is optional street parking on Portrero Dr/Wendy Dr. Follow the Los Robles connector trail east .5 miles to access the trailhead.

*Elevation and mileage are approximate.

Overview: This route is an out and back. Elevation shows round trip. This trail is used mainly by hikers and mountain bikers. The trail connects Los Robles Tr to Point Mugu State Park. Los Robles Tr begins at a pretty, quaint dirt parking lot on the east end of Potrero Rd. The parking lot doesn't get crowded on the weekends and is equipped with a picnic table, drinking fountain, and a horse waterer. The parking lot is open daily from 9–4. There is additional parking .5 mile west on Potrero Rd/Wendy Dr, following Los Robles Connector Tr east to the trailhead. **(1)** The route begins as a pleasant single track gradually winding through chaparral and coastal sage scrub alongside some houses heading north 1.3 miles. There is some poison oak on this section of the trail. **(2)** Right turn at the junction on the Los Robles Tr 1.5 miles to Angel Vista. The trail becomes steep ascending and descending approximately three steep hills traveling east alongside partially fenced private land. The footing along the edges of the trail is hard packed and sloped with

Angel Vista with views of the Conejo Valley

Los Robles Tr

Potrero Road to Angel Vista

a rut in the center of the trail filled with loose rocks. The edges of the trail can be slick. Walking sticks are recommended for this hike. The last portion of the trail is a pleasant gradual single track winding up to the top traveling north joining the Los Robles West Tr. (a.k.a. Space Mountain). It is a very popular mountain biking trail. **(3)** Left turn (northwest) .1 mile. You will pass a junction to the right. Stay uphill until you reach the benches. You will see many mountain bikers on this short section. There are two picnic benches at the top; usually an ocean breeze; views of the Channel Islands, Hidden Valley, Point Mugu State Park, and Ventura on a clear day.

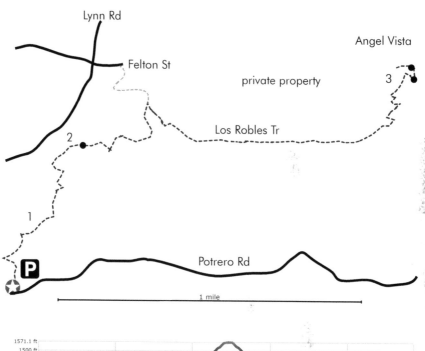

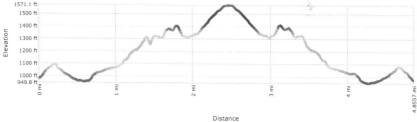

Triunfo Park/Potrero Road 🚴 🚶 🐎

Highlights:	Triunfo Cyn Tr to the Los Robles Trail from Thousand Oaks to Newbury Park
Miles:	10.3 miles one way; 20.6 miles round trip
Elevation:	1950 ft one way; 3800 ft. out and back
Estimated time:	biking: 1.5-2.5 hrs one way
	hiking and horseback riding: 3-4 hrs
Technical:	★★★⯨☆
Aerobic:	★★★★☆
Restrooms:	yes
Water:	drinking fountains
Dogs:	on leash
Parking:	Triunfo Community Park, Potrero Rd is free

Directions to Trailhead: GPS 34.15621,-118.846648
980 Aranmoor Ave Triunfo Community Park, Thousand Oaks
101 Fwy: exit 40 for CA-23 S. South onto Westlake Blvd. Right on Triunfo Cyn Rd. Left on Tamarack St. It is on the corner of Tamarack St and Aranmoor Ave.
*Elevation and mileage are approximate.

Overview: This trail is an out-and-back. Elevation includes round trip. A car can be left at each trailhead, or for an easier trip back to Triunfo, make a left on Potrero Rd. Left on Westlake Blvd. Left on Triunfo Cyn Rd. The park is equipped with restrooms, drinking fountain, tennis courts, picnic tables, soccer fields, ada parking, BBQ grills, basketball courts, and volleyball courts. The park hours are 7 am–10 pm. There is additional street parking. The other trailhead is on Potrero Rd in Newbury Park equipped with a picnic table, drinking fountain, and automatic horse waterer. The parking lot is behind gates and the hours are 9–4. There is additional street parking .5 mile west on Potrero Dr/Wendy Dr. Follow the Los Robles Connector Tr east to the trailhead. The hills are moderate with a .75 mile hike-a-bike steep section each way. The Los Robles West section is a popular mountain bike trail with blind turns and drop offs. The trailhead is next to the 2nd parking lot near the volleyball courts. **(1)** Begin at the trailhead closest to Tamarack St. The Triunfo Cyn single track pleasantly winds up the canyon on a rocky trail 1.1 miles. **(2)** Left at the junction on the Los Robles Tr as the wide trail gradually ascends and descends 2.2 miles. **(3)** After meandering along the moderate trail along the meadow,

The bench off of Los Robles Tr

Triunfo Park to Potrero Road

left down the canyon .6 mile. **(4)** At the junction with a bench under an oak tree, continue straight down the wide trail .5 mile. **(5)** At the next split, left turn .1 mile. **(6)** Left on Los Robles West 3 miles. The single track is a popular mountain biking trail. The trail has embedded rocks and many switchback as it gradually climbs up and down the canyon. Follow signs for Portrero Rd. There are "No Trespassing" signs, so please stay on the trail. For a rest, continue past the next two junctions .1 mile to the end of the trail at Angel Vista for a beautiful rest/view spot. **(7)** To continue, head back down the way you came to the first junction on the right, right down the Los Robles Tr southwest 1.5 miles. The trail begins with a gradual grade and sweeping turns leading to steep rutted hills ascending and descending. The trail is slippery so walking sticks are recommended. **(8)** At the next junction left 1.3 miles on the rolling trail with gradual turns and grade leading to Portrero Dr.

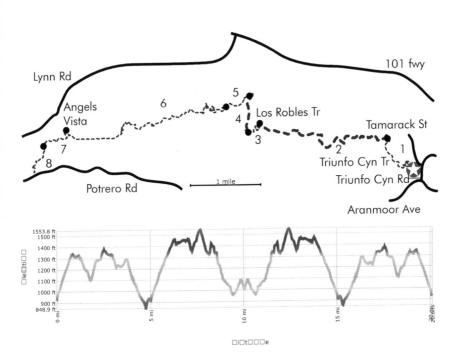

Triunfo Park/ Los Robles Trail

Highlights: Climb from Triunfo Community Park to Los Robles Tr overlook with 360 views
Miles: 5 miles
Elevation: 1000 ft
Estimated time: biking: 45 mins+
hiking and horseback riding: 1-2 hrs
Technical: ★★★✦☆
Aerobic: ★★★✦☆
Restrooms: yes
Water: drinking fountain
Dogs: on leash
Parking: Triunfo Community Park parking lot

Directions to Trailhead: GPS 34.15621,-118.846648
980 Aranmoor Ave Triunfo Community Park, Thousand Oaks
101 fwy: exit 40 for CA-23 S. South onto Westlake Blvd. Right onto Triunfo Cyn Rd. Left on Tamarack St. It is on the corner of Tamarack St and Aranmoor Ave.
*Elevation and mileage are approximate.

Overview: The park is equipped with restrooms, a drinking fountain, tennis courts, picnic tables, soccer fields, ada parking, BBQ grills, basketball courts, volleyball courts, and play equipment. There are a couple parking lots, the trailhead is next to the second parking lot near the volleyball courts. The park hours are 7 am–10 pm. There is additional street parking. The street is wide and flat and can accommodate a horse trailer. This loop has a lot of climbing up and down loose rocky hills, winding around twisty trails through the canyons with lake views. The majority of this loop is non-technical, with .2 miles of steep single track and rocky terrain. Begin at the trailhead near the volleyball courts. **(1)** Follow the Triunfo Cyn Tr 1.2 miles. The trail gradually winds up the canyon leading to a T. This is a popular hiking and running trail. **(2)** Right turn on Los Robles Tr .2 miles to the next junction. **(3)** At the intersection stay to the right down the fire road and back up with lake views. The trail drops back down the hill and turns into a single track .7 mile. At the next junction, there is an option to take the left turn down the single track leading to Los Robles Tr. This would shorten the ride approximately .5 mile

Triunfo Park/Los Robles Trail

and avoid the loose rocky section. For the next .2 mile the trail becomes loose, steep, and rocky. The trail scales above houses for a short time heading west. **(4)** Left at the junction on Los Robles Tr 1 mile up the gradual hill with firm, smooth footing. **(5)** Drop down and up a hill .2 mile. **(6)** Just past the turn off to Triunfo Park is another junction. Slight Left up the steep rocky hill .2 mile. At the top turn left. There are stairs leading to a 360 view with a bench. **(7)** Continue downhill .2 mile. **(8)** Turn left for 10 ft connecting back to the Triunfo Cyn Tr. Right .9 mile back to the parking lot.

Willow Ln

Foothill Dr

Fairview Rd

4

5

Los Robles Tr

Los Robles Tr

2

steep, loose rocks

3

6

7

Tamarack St

Antares Ct

Triunfo Canyon Tr

8   1

Triunfo Canyon Rd

0.50 miles

1437.1 ft
1400 ft
1300 ft
1200 ft
1100 ft
1000 ft
900 ft
834.7 ft

0 mi   1 mi   2 mi   3 mi   4 mi   4.761 mi

202

Top of Los Robles Tr

Wildwood Regional Park

Conejo Open Space Conservation agency
Conejo Recreation and Park District

Located at the west section of Thousand Oaks at the end of Avenida De Los Arboles, Wildwood Regional Park includes 1,700 acres of open space abutting 1400 additional acres of open space. The incredible varied terrain from areas of cactus and volcanic rock outcroppings to trails with lush sycamore trees running alongside the year-round creek makes this area a special place to visit. The 37-ft Paradise Falls waterfall seems to be the main feature of the park. The falls attracts local residents as well as bus loads of school children for educational tours during the week. Most trails are multi-use, although some trails are designated for hiking only. There is a picnic bench and drinking fountain at the parking area. There are restrooms, a drinking fountain, hitching posts, and picnic tables at the Wildwood Cyn Tr/Lizard Rock intersection, and a restroom towards the Nature Center across the bridge. Hiking, mountain biking, and horseback riding are common activities in the park. Many of these loops can be linked together. Weekends and holidays get very crowded. In the summer the temperature can get hot; yet, the park is usually a few degrees cooler than surrounding areas because there is an ocean breeze. After a rain much of the area stays wet and the mud sticks to bike tires.

Wildwood Cyn Tr

Paradise Falls Loop

Highlights:	37-ft waterfall and water crossings with lush vegetation to a climb up switchbacks
Miles:	4.3 miles
Elevation:	700 ft
Estimated time:	biking: 45 mins-1 hr
	hiking & horseback riding: 1.5 hrs
Technical:	★★★⯪☆
Aerobic:	★★★⯪☆
Restrooms:	in the park
Water:	drinking fountain in parking lot
Dogs:	on leash
Parking:	dirt parking lot is free

Directions to Trailhead: GPS 34.22008,-118.902926
Avenida De Los Arboles,Thousand Oaks
23 Fwy: exit 15 Avenida De Los Arboles .2 mile. West on Avenida De Los Arboles 3.4 miles. The dirt parking lot is on the corner of Avenida De Los Arboles/Big Sky Dr.
*Elevation and mileage are approximate.

Overview: This is a popular loop for hikers, mountain bikers, and equestrians. Paradise Falls is a popular destination in the summer for field trips, on the weekends, and holidays. The footing is hard packed and uneven with rocks. The grade is moderate. **(1)** Begin at the flat Mesa Tr south .3 mile along a grassy meadow with cactus on the hillsides. **(2)** At the first junction, left down the Public Access Tr .7 mile along the wide trail. (There are restrooms and a drinking fountain across the bridge and to the left.) **(3)** Right on the Wildwood Cyn Tr .6 mile over the waterfall and through the water crossings. The footing becomes rocky at this point. There is a chain link fence when you are above the waterfall. The water crossings have small floating bridges if needed for hikers and mountain bikers. The roots of the trees can become slippery when wet. Left at the junction above the waterfall, down the hill along the wooden fence rail, and continue right at the bottom along the flat sycamore-shaded trail passing the picnic areas. **(4)** The next junction is Lizard Rock Tr 1.4 miles. Stay slight left past the restrooms and the trail becomes Lizard Rock Tr. The trail narrows and becomes rocky climbing up the switchbacks and past the water treatment plant. When passing the water treatment plant there can be a smell depending on the direction of

Wildwood Cyn Tr across the bridge

Paradise Falls waterfall area

Paradise Falls Loop

the wind, but the trail is still worth doing. After passing the treatment plant, there are scenic views of Santa Rosa Valley to the west for the duration of the climb. **(5)** Head down the trail 1.1 miles. There is a fence along the steep section .2 mile. The trail gently levels off for 1 mile leading back to the parking lot.

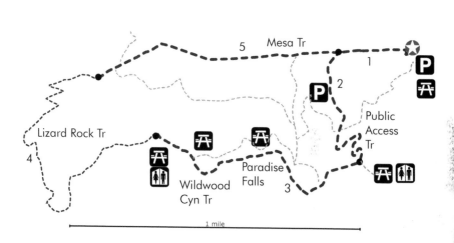

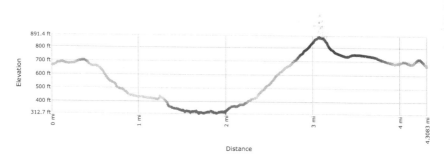

Lynnmere/Stagecoach Trail 🚴 🚶 🏇

Highlights: Mostly single track with many water crossings, a climb up switchbacks ending with a technical challenge on a rocky plateau; 1 mile of street

Miles: 7.1 miles

Elevation: 1200 ft

Estimated time: biking: 1- 1.5 hrs
hiking and horseback riding: 3 hrs

Technical: ★★★✦☆

Aerobic: ★★★✦☆

Restrooms: in the park

Water: drinking fountain in parking lot and in park

Dogs: on leash

Parking: dirt parking lot is free

Directions to Trailhead: GPS 34.22008,-118.902926
Avenida De Los Arboles, Thousand Oaks
23 Fwy: exit 15 Avenida De Los Arboles .2 mile. West on Avenida De Los Arboles 3.4 miles. The dirt parking lot is on the corner of Avenida De Los Arboles/Big Sky Dr.
*Elevation and mileage are approximate.

Overview: This is a popular trail suitable for hikers, horseback riders and intermediate mountain bike riders. The footing is hard packed, uneven footing with rocks. The hills are moderate with steep sections. Equestrians can do a reverse out and back turning around at Lynn Rd to avoid street travel. **(1)** The loop begins with .8 mile on Avenida De Los Arboles. Right turn on Lynn Road .4 mile. Passed Avenida De Las Flores there will be a trail alongside a fence. **(2)** Right on the Lynnmere single track trail in and out of the canyons rolling through coastal sage scrub and crossing a couple of bridges heading west 2 miles. The trail is a moderate grade with a couple of steep sections. **3)** You will come to an intersection with a small bridge. Right at the junction .5 mile descending down the hill. **(4)** Cross the water, left on Wildwood Canyon Tr .6 mile traveling along the wide flat trail and over the waterfall. There is a chain link fence alongside the edge of the waterfall. The water crossings have small floating bridges if needed for hikers and mountain bikers. **(5)** At the junction, turn left down the hill and continue right at the bottom away from the waterfall along the flat sycamore shaded trail through the picnic areas. **(6)** The next junction is Lizard

Lynnmere Tr

Top of Lizard Rock Tr

Rock Tr. Stay straight onto Lizard Rock Tr 1.4 miles. Travel past the water treatment plant climbing up switchbacks leading to panoramic views. The trail narrows and becomes rocky on Lizard Rock Tr. **(7)** Head down the trail for .2 mile. **(8)** At the next junction right turn on Stage Coach Tr. This is a fun, rocky, technical trail with a couple steep sections. It is .7 mile, but feels like much more. **(9)** Left turn on N Tepee Tr .2 mile. When the trail drops down a steep hill and comes to a T, right turn on Mesa Tr. **(10)** When the trail splits and begins to ascend up a hill, either direction will take you back to the parking lot .3 mile. The Public Access Rd to the right is flat.

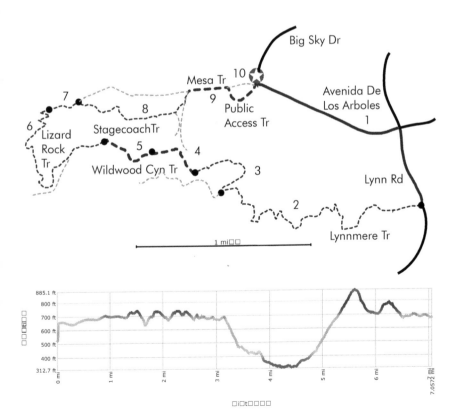

Box Canyon to Lower Butte 🚴 🥾 🐎

Highlights:	A descent down to Santa Rosa Valley climbing up switchbacks over volcanic rock and among cactus and grassy hillsides; views
Miles:	6.6 miles
Elevation:	1000 ft
Estimated time:	biking: 1-1.5 hrs
	hiking and horseback riding: 2-2.5 hrs
Technical:	★★★★☆
Aerobic:	★★★☆☆
Restrooms:	in the park
Water:	drinking fountain
Dogs:	on leash
Parking:	Wildwood dirt parking lot is free

Directions to Trailhead: GPS 34.22008,-118.902926
Avenida De Los Arboles, Thousand Oaks
23 Fwy: exit 15 for Avenida De Los Arboles. West on Avenida De Los Arboles 3.4 miles. It is on the corner of Avenida De Los Arboles/Big Sky Drive.
*Elevation and mileage are approximate.

Overview: This loop is an option for those who don't want to ride along the narrow trail among the cactus on Upper Santa Rosa Tr. This trail is a great get away from crowds and suitable for hikers, equestrians, and mountain bikers. The footing is hard packed, loose rocks; the hills are mostly moderate with a couple steep hills. There is a low tunnel; equestrians should dismount before entering the tunnel. **(1)** Begin traveling south from Wildwood parking lot on the Public Accesss Tr .3 mile. Left on Mesa Tr .6 mile along the mesa. **(2)** Right turn ascending down Box Canyon Tr. After 300 ft. right at the junction 1 mile. **(3)** You will end up on Rocky High Rd .3 mile. **(4)** Talap Ct is the next junction. There is a single track trail to the right. Follow lower Santa Rosa Tr 1.1 miles as you travel along the base of the hillside east. The trail has a moderate grade except for two steep sections. You will pass by farm land to the north. **(5)** Turn right at the next junction on Shooting Star Tr 1.1 miles up the moderate grade and firm footing. There are tight switchbacks and small embedded volcanic rocks. **(6)** Left on Santa Rosa Tr .2 mile where the trail climbs up a steep rocky section. **(7)** Follow signs for Lower Butte Tr .8 mile southwest towards Wildwood Ave. Go over the stepover.

Box Cyn Tr

Santa Rosa Tr

It passes along houses and climbs a hill. **(8)** Left on Wildwood Ave .4 mile. The sidewalk turns into a dirt sidewalk on the east side of the street. **(9)** Cross at the crosswalk, south on Olsen Channel Tr .6 mile as it parallels the Olsen Channel. Just before the tunnel, the trail goes around a fence. Continue the same direction with the tennis courts on your left. Towards the end of the Olsen Channel Tr. There is a tunnel that travels underneath Avenida De Los Arboles. The tunnel is low on the sides near the bottom. Equestrians should dismount and hand walk their horse through the tunnel. There is an option to walk to the street and continue on Avenida De Los Arboles or pick up the trail across the street. **(10)** Right after the tunnel. Right on the Indian Creek Tr .2 mile as it parallels Avenida De Los Arboles. Do not go down the canyon on Indian Creek Tr if traveling by horseback. There are low hanging branches, steps, and slippery rocks. **(11)** Just before the parking lot, the trail makes a sharp left with steps leading to the parking lot. Horses should take the right just before the left turn leading to Avenida De Los Arboles for 10 ft to the parking lot.

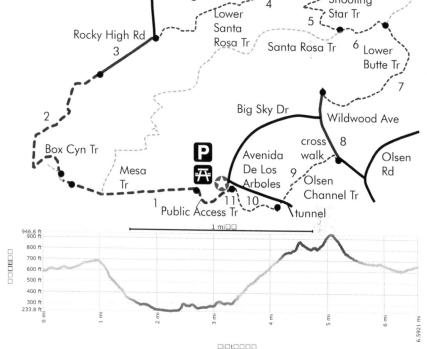

Santa Rosa Trail/ Lower Butte

Highlights:	Climb up switchbacks among cactus and along the edge of a hillside with views of Santa Rosa Valley maneuvering over volcanic rock.
Miles:	4 miles
Elevation:	700 ft
Estimated time:	biking: 1-1.5 hrs
	hiking and horseback riding: 3 hrs
Technical:	★★★★☆
Aerobic:	★★★☆☆
Restrooms:	in the park
Water:	drinking fountain
Dogs:	on leash
Parking:	dirt parking lot is free

Directions to Trailhead: GPS 34.22008,-118.902926
Avenida De Los Arboles, Thousand Oaks
23 Fwy: exit 15 Avenida De Los Arboles .2 mile. West on Avenida De Los Arboles 3.4 mile. The dirt parking lot is on the corner of Avenida De Los Arboles/Big Sky Dr.
*Elevation and mileage are approximate.

Overview: Mesa Tr and Santa Rosa Tr are active trails in the park. Many people turn back at the top of the Santa Rosa Tr. Santa Rosa Tr is a steep rocky trail among cactus that climbs up steep switchbacks leading to views of the Santa Rosa Valley. The footing is loose in sections and the cactus is very close to the edges of the trail. The remainder of the trail is rocky; the volcanic rocks on the Santa Rosa Tr makes the trail challenging for mountain bikers. **(1)** Beginning at the main parking lot, head south on the Mesa Tr. .3 miles. This trail is relatively flat along a meadow. **(2)** Right up the switchbacks on the Santa Rosa Tr .7 mile. Right at the first split leading up to the top with views of Santa Rosa Valley. **(3)** Continue straight along the rocky hillside with a gentle grade 1.5 miles. Pass through the intersections and continue along the hillside. The trail bends to the right ending with a steep, rocky hill. You will end up next to a neighborhood on Camino de Celeste. Stay straight, cross the stepover, and continue in between the houses. **(4)** Follow signs for Lower Butte Tr .8 mile southwest towards Wildwood Ave. Go over

Santa Rosa Trail/Lower Butte

the stepover. This trail passes along houses and climbs a hill. **(5)** Left on Wildwood Ave .4 mile. The cement sidewalk turns into a dirt sidewalk on the east side of the street. **(6)** Cross at the crosswalk, south on Olsen Channel Tr .6 mile as it parallels the Olsen Channel. Just before the tunnel, the trail goes around a fence. Continue the same direction with the tennis courts on your left. Towards the end of the Olsen Channel Tr there is a tunnel that travels underneath Avenida De Los Arboles. The tunnel is low on the sides near the bottom. Equestrians should dismount and hand walk their horse through the tunnel. There is an option to walk to the street and continue on Avenida De Los Arboles or pick up the trail across the street. **(7)** Right after the tunnel. Right on the Indian Creek Tr. The trail bends around towards Wildwood Creek Tr .2 mile as it parallels Avenida De Los Arboles. Do not go down the canyon on Indian Creek Tr if traveling by horseback or bike. There are low hanging branches,

Santa Rosa Tr

215

steps, and slippery rocks. Just before the parking lot, the trail makes a sharp left with steps leading to the parking lot. Horses should take the right just before the parking lot leading to Avenida De Los Arboles for 10 ft to the parking lot.

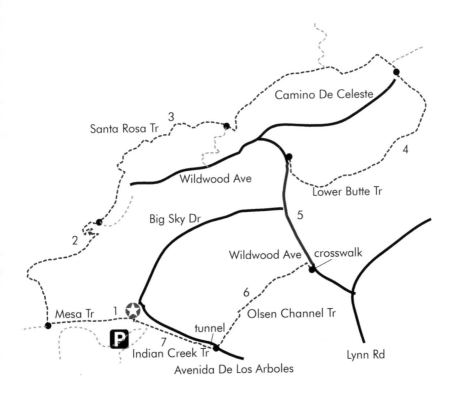

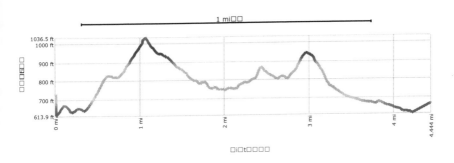

Topanga State Park/Westridge Canyonback Wilderness Park/ San Vicente Mountain Park

Santa Monica Mountains Conservation Agency
Mountains Recreation and Conservation Authority

NOTE: The MRCA has installed hidden cameras at the stop signs near the top of Reseda Blvd at the Marvin Braude Mulholland Gateway Park, the Top of Topanga Overlook, Frankin Canyon Park, and the Temescal Gateway Park. The fines are $100-$175.

Topanga State Park is located in Los Angeles on the east end of the Santa Monica Mountains with approximately 36 miles of trails through rustic canyons, coastal sage scrub and live oaks with views of the ocean. The park is a busy attraction especially on weekends and holidays. The parking lot fills up quickly. Parking is $10 at the Trippet Ranch main entrance. Hours of operation are 8 am–dusk. Camping is allowed at the park. Contact the park directly for information 310-455-2465. Dogs are not allowed in Topanga State Park.

Westridge Canyonback Wilderness Park is located east of Topanga State Park with 1500 acres of open space. Dogs are permitted off leash under their owner's immediate control. http://www.lamountains.com/parks_dogs.asp. The park can be accessed in the San Fernando Valley from San Vicente Park in Encino, and from Westridge Trailhead in Pacific Palisades. San Vicente Mountain Park is located adjacent to Topanga State Park and Westridge Canyonback Wilderness including 10.2 acres offering 360 degree views, picnic areas, restrooms, and access to a large network of trails.

Mulholland Drive runs east and west along the ridgetop with panoramic views. Temescal Ridge Trail, Eagle Springs Fire Road, Westridge Fire Road, East Topanga Fire Road and Rogers Road (Backbone Trail) run north and south.

This area can get hot in the summer and there isn't much shade. There are drinking fountains and restrooms at the main entrance as well as the Hub junction at the intersection of Eagle Springs and Fire Rd #30, at San Vicente Mountain Park, and at Marvin Braude Mulholland Gateway Park at the top of Reseda Blvd.

Caballero Canyon/Sullivan 🚴 🥾 🐎 Canyon/Westridge Trail

Highlights:	Scenic climb up the canyon with a long gradual descent on a shaded trail
Miles:	16.3 miles
Elevation:	2500 ft
Estimated time:	biking: 2+hrs hiking and horseback riding: 4+hrs
Technical:	★★★☆☆
Aerobic:	★★★½☆
Restrooms:	San Vicente Mountain Park
Water:	drinking fountain- San Vicente Mountain Park
Dogs:	no - Topanga State Park, yes - Westridge Canyonback
Parking:	street parking is free

Directions to Trailhead: GPS 34.142731,-118.540834
Caballero Canyon Trailhead, Reseda Blvd, Encino
101 Fwy: exit Reseda Blvd. Head south for 2 miles. Trailhead is on the east side of the street just before Country Club Pl.
*Elevation and mileage are approximate.

Overview: Reseda Blvd has a slight grade and is wide enough to accommodate a horse trailer and to turn it around. The trails are a combination of non-technical wide-open fire roads with full sun exposure, a shaded single track trail, and a partially rutted single track trail. The grade is moderate with firm and loose footing and rocky sections. The route is good for hiking, mountain biking, and horseback riding. There is 1 mile of residential street riding. To avoid street travel, turn around at the end of Sullivan Cyn Tr. Dogs are allowed on the Westridge Fire Road only. There is parking at the end of Westridge Rd in Pacific Palisades and Encino Blvd. **(1)** Begin on Reseda Blvd at the Caballero Cyn trailhead. Follow the trail along the canyon floor through the wash. There will be a few trails meandering off of the main trail; stay to the right along the trail with some ruts for a short time before ascending up the canyon. This trail is popular with hikers and mountain bikers. After 1.4 miles you will come to Mulholland Dr. **(2)** Left on Mulholland 1.7 miles. **(3)** Right turn on Sullivan Cyn Tr. The trail name is on the gate, but it does fade. There is a sign on the opposite side of the trail that reads San Vicente Park .7 mile.

Caballero Canyon/Sullivan Canyon/Westridge Trail

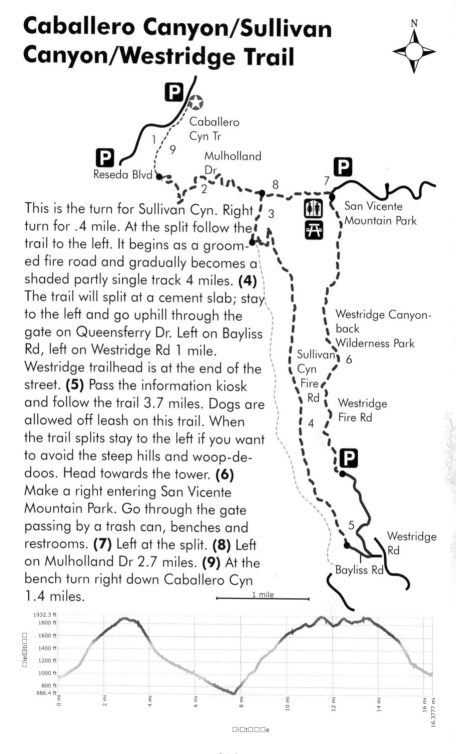

N

Caballero Cyn Tr

Mulholland Dr

Reseda Blvd

San Vicente Mountain Park

This is the turn for Sullivan Cyn. Right turn for .4 mile. At the split follow the trail to the left. It begins as a groomed fire road and gradually becomes a shaded partly single track 4 miles. **(4)** The trail will split at a cement slab; stay to the left and go uphill through the gate on Queensferry Dr. Left on Bayliss Rd, left on Westridge Rd 1 mile. Westridge trailhead is at the end of the street. **(5)** Pass the information kiosk and follow the trail 3.7 miles. Dogs are allowed off leash on this trail. When the trail splits stay to the left if you want to avoid the steep hills and woop-de-doos. Head towards the tower. **(6)** Make a right entering San Vicente Mountain Park. Go through the gate passing by a trash can, benches and restrooms. **(7)** Left at the split. **(8)** Left on Mulholland Dr 2.7 miles. **(9)** At the bench turn right down Caballero Cyn 1.4 miles.

Westridge Canyon-back Wilderness Park

Sullivan Cyn Fire Rd

Westridge Fire Rd

Westridge Rd

Bayliss Rd

1 mile

Caballero Cyn Tr

Backbone Trail to Will Rogers State Park

Highlights:	Wide open fireroad leading to a single track; ocean views leading to Will Rogers State Park
Miles:	10.3 miles one way; 20.6 miles round trip
Elevation:	3400 ft total elevation
Estimated time:	biking: 3+hrs
	hiking and horseback riding: 4+hrs
Technical:	★★✦☆☆
Aerobic:	★★★★☆
Restrooms:	Trippet Ranch, The Hub, Will Rogers State Park
Water:	Trippet Ranch, Will Rogers State Park
Dogs:	no
Parking:	Trippet Ranch Parking lot is $10

Directions to Trailhead: GPS 34.093388,-118.587724
20829 Entrada Rd, Topanga Canyon
Follow Topanga Canyon Blvd. East on Entrada Rd. Left turns to stay on Entrada Rd. Exiting the state park, horse trailers should make a left turn heading south on Topanga Canyon Blvd. There is not enough room to turn right.
*Elevation and mileage are approximate.

Overview: This route is an out-and-back following the Backbone single track trail dropping down to Will Rogers State Park with ocean views. The footing varies with firm, smooth, and loose with rocks. The elevation graph shows one way. There is a 300–ft section just past the view point above Will Rogers State Park to walk your bike because the trail becomes narrow, steep, and rocky. **(1)** Begin from the Trippet Ranch Parking lot follow the trail towards Eagle Springs Fire Rd .3 mile. **(2)** Left on Eagle Springs Fire Rd 1.2 miles. **(3)** Right at the split 1.3 miles leading to Hub Junction. There is a porta potty and a shade area. **(4)** Right turn on the fire road .6 mile. **(5)** Left on Backbone Tr 6 miles. This trail has sweeping turns with a gradual grade. The trail gets steeper and rockier for the last mile. At the end of the Backbone trail, you will be in Will Rogers State Park. **(6)** Left on the Loop Tr on a wide groomed trail leading to the polo fields .9 mile. Will Rogers State Park offers WI FI service within 150 ft of the Rangers Station, green grass for a picnic, restrooms, and barbecues. Turn around and return the way we came.

View from Backbone Tr

Backbone Trail to Will Rogers State Park

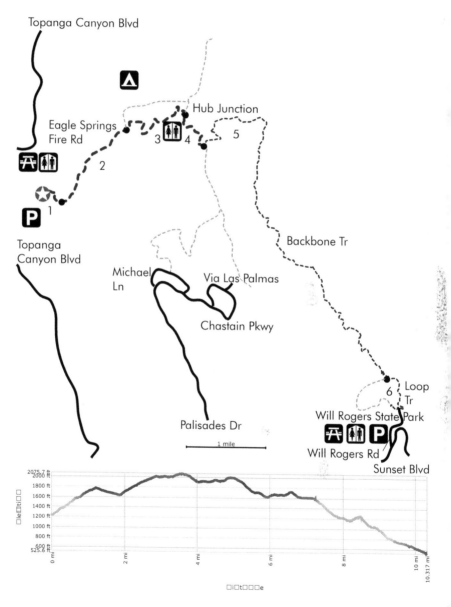

Topanga Canyon Blvd

Eagle Springs
Fire Rd

2

Hub Junction

3   4   5

Topanga
Canyon Blvd

P   1

Backbone Tr

Michael
Ln

Via Las Palmas

Chastain Pkwy

Palisades Dr

1 mile

Loop
Tr   6

Will Rogers State Park

Will Rogers Rd

Sunset Blvd

2075.7 ft 2000 ft
1800 ft
1600 ft
1400 ft
1200 ft
1000 ft
800 ft
600 ft
525.6 ft

0 mi   2 mi   4 mi   6 mi   8 mi   10 mi   10.317 mi

Temescal Ridge Fire Road/ 🚴 🧗 🏇
East Topanga Fire Road

Highlights:	Wide open fireroad with ocean views skirting the edge of the park
Miles:	16 miles
Elevation:	2600 ft
Estimated time:	biking: 2+hrs hiking and horseback riding: 4+hrs
Technical:	★★☆☆☆
Aerobic:	★★★☆☆
Restrooms:	yes
Water:	drinking fountain
Dogs:	no
Parking:	street parking is free

Directions to Trailhead: GPS 34.078683,-118.559915
Trailer Canyon Trailhead, Michael Lane, Pacific Palisades
Sunset Blvd: West on Palisades Dr 2.4 miles. Left on Vereda de La Montura. Right on Michael Ln. Trail is on the left side of the street.
*Elevation and mileage are approximate.

Overview: There are four miles of street riding to connect the trails to do the entire loop. There is limited street parking on steep, narrow streets in Pacific Palisades. **(1)** Begin at Trailer Canyon trailhead on Michael Lane. Head north 4.4 miles up Temescal Ridge Trail with a moderate grade. You will pass a split at 2 miles and the backbone turn off. Continue to the Hub junction with a restroom and shade area. **(2)** Left at the junction 1.3 miles. **(3)** At the next split left on Eagle Springs Fire Rd 1 mile. (There is a turn off to the right leading to the main entrance with restooms and a drinking fountain.) Continue along East Topanga Fire Road 2.5 miles to the split. The trail to the right leads to Parker Mesa Overlook. Continue on the fire road stay to the left at the split 2.1 miles. The trail is steep downhill with stunning coastal views leading to Paseo Miramar. **(4)** Follow the Paseo Miramar down the steep hill, and left on Sunset Blvd. Left on Palisades Dr. Left on Vereda de La Montura. Right on Michael Lane.

E Topanga Fire Rd

Temescal Ridge Fire Road/
East Topanga Fire Road

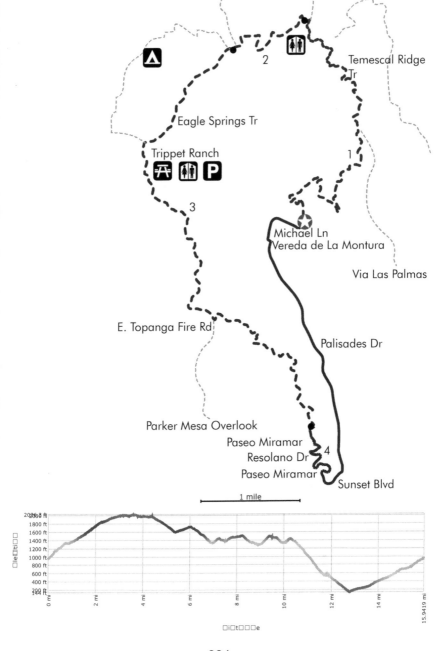

Temescal Ridge Tr

Eagle Springs Tr

Trippet Ranch

1

2

3

Michael Ln
Vereda de La Montura

Via Las Palmas

Palisades Dr

E. Topanga Fire Rd

Parker Mesa Overlook

Paseo Miramar

Resolano Dr

Paseo Miramar

4

Sunset Blvd

1 mile

Serrania Park to Caballero Canyon Trail

Highlights:	Begin up a steep, technical single track; along Mulholland Dr and drop into a scenic canyon
Miles:	11.4 miles
Elevation:	1830 ft
Estimated time:	biking: 1.5+hrs
	hiking and horseback riding: 3 hrs
Technical:	★★★★☆
Aerobic:	★★★★☆
Restrooms:	yes
Water:	drinking fountain
Dogs:	no
Parking:	parking lot is free

Directions to Trailhead: GPS 34.157504,-118.585535
Serrania Park, 20864 Wells Dr, Woodland Hills 818-883-9370
101 Fwy: exit De Soto. Head south approximately 1 mile. Pass the school. The park is on the right side.
*Elevation and mileage are approximate.

Overview: There is approximately one mile of street travel on Reseda Blvd to the trailhead at the end of the street. There is a sidewalk along Reseda Blvd. There is a small parking lot and street parking available. Beginning on Wells Dr, the path is on the side of the park. The park is equipped with restrooms, picnic tables, and a drinking fountain.

Single track from Serrania Park

Serrania Park to Caballero Canyon Trail

(1) It begins as a wide trail, and ascends and descends quickly with a steep technical climb 1.1 miles. The trail branches off; stay on the main trail heading south. **(2)** Left on Mulholland Dr with a moderate grade 3.7 miles. **(3)** Left down Caballero Cyn Tr 1.4 miles. This trail has ruts and is steep in sections. There are a couple short sections where there is a drop and the trail is a few feet wide. This is a fun trail. **(4)** Once you are on the street, left turn up Reseda Blvd to the trailhead 1.2 miles. There is parking, restrooms, drinking fountain, and trash cans. **(5)** Pass the trailhead sign. You can take the wide trail or the single track .2 mile to the right. They both lead to Mulholland Dr. **(6)** Right on Mulholland Dr 2.7 miles. **(7)** Look for a sign on the right just past private property across the street. Follow the steep technical single track down the hill to Serrania Park 1.1 miles.

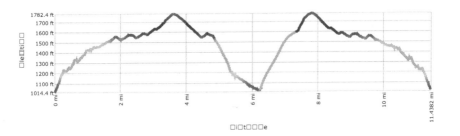

Mulholland Drive to San Vicente Mountain Park

Highlights: Wide open fireroad with views; family trail
Miles: 3.6 miles one way; 7.2 miles round trip
Elevation: 800 ft total elevation
Estimated time: biking: 1+hrs
hiking and horseback riding: 2+hrs
Technical: ★★☆☆☆
Aerobic: ★★⯪☆☆
Restrooms: yes
Water: yes
Dogs: no
Parking: street parking is free; optional parking is $5

Directions to Trailhead: GPS 34.131269,-118.553118
Marvin Braude Mulholland Gateway Park, Reseda Blvd, Encino
101 Fwy: exit Reseda Blvd. South 3 miles to the end of the road.
*Elevation and mileage are approximate.

Overview:

NOTE: The MRCA has installed a hidden camera at the stop sign near the top of Reseda Blvd at the Marvin Braude Mulholland Gateway Park. The fine for running the stop sign is $100-175.

Parking is free on the lower portion of Reseda Blvd before the yellow line. Parking spots above the yellow line are on a flatter section of the road in the fee area. Cost is $5 near the trailhead. Cash or check can be inserted in the box. This is a good place to park a horse trailer. There is a turn around at the end of the street. There are restrooms, a drinking fountain, and trash can.

To access the $5 parking, you will pass through the stop sign with the hidden camera to access the section of Reseda Blvd that is recommended for horse trailers. You must stop at the stop sign to avoid a ticket!

This trail is good for novice mountain bikers, horseback riders, and hikers. The area gets hot in the summer time with no shade until you reach San Vicente Mountain Park.

View from Mulholland Dr

Mulholland Drive to San Vicente Mountain Park

This route is good for families. The grade is moderate and the trail is wide. There are panoramic views along Mulholland Dr leading to a rest area with restrooms, picnic tables, drinking fountain, and a viewing tower. **(1)** Head up the trail from Reseda Blvd leading to Mulholland Dr .2 mile. **(2)** Turn left on Mulholland Dr 3 mile. Head towards the tower. **(3)** Turn right along the fence leading to San Vicente Park. Return the way you came.

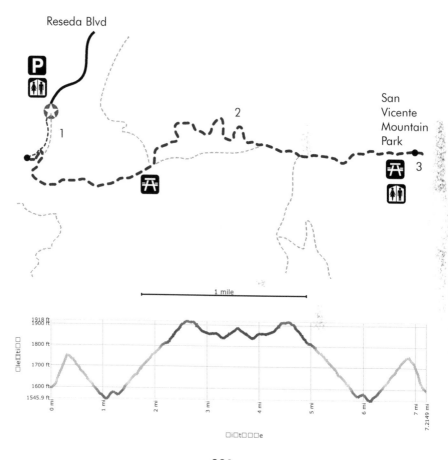

Caballero Canyon/
Sullivan Canyon Loop

Highlights:	Climb up Caballero Cyn leading to panoramic views; down an open fire road, and a climb back up a lush shaded trail
Miles:	14 miles
Elevation:	2177 ft
Estimated time:	biking: 2+hrs hiking and horseback riding: 4+hrs
Technical:	★★★☆☆
Aerobic:	★★★⯪☆
Restrooms:	no
Water:	no
Dogs:	no
Parking:	street parking is free

Directions to Trailhead: GPS 34.142731,-118.540834
Caballero Canyon Trailhead, Reseda Blvd, Encino
101 Fwy: exit Reseda Blvd. Head south for 2 miles. Trailhead is on the east side of the street just before Country Club Pl.
*Elevation and mileage are approximate.

Overview: This is one of my favorite rides in Topanga. On the weekends it can be crowded with hikers and mountain bikers. Reseda Blvd is on a slight grade and wide enough to accommodate a horse trailer and to turn it around. The grade is moderate, and the footing varies from soft and firm to rocky in places. There is some shade on the Sullivan Cyn Tr. The ride is good for hiking, mountain biking and horseback riding and can be ridden in either direction. **(1)** Begin on Reseda Blvd at the Caballero Cyn trailhead. Follow the trail along the canyon floor through the wash. There will be a few trails meandering off of the main trail; stay to the right along the trail for a short time before ascending up the canyon. There are some ruts in the trail to maneuver around. After 1.4 miles you will come to Mulholland Dr. **(2)** Left on Mulholland Dr 1.7 miles. **(3)** Right turn on Sullivan Cyn Tr. The trail name is on the gate, but it does fade. There is a sign on the opposite side of the trail that reads San Vicente Park .7 mile. This is Sullivan Cyn. Right turn for 3.4 miles, stay straight past the turn off. You will be returning on that trail. At the bottom of the hill go around a gate. You will end

Sullivan Cyn Tr

Caballero Canyon/
Sullivan Canyon Loop

up on pavement for a short time. Keep an eye out for a single track on the left side. It is next to a pole. **(4)** Follow the goat trail .2 mile. The trail is steep and loose with rocks. Walking your bike is recommended on most of this trail. **(5)**Left turn on Sullivan Canyon Fire Rd. 3.2 miles along the lush shaded trail. Left at the split .4 mile. Right on Sullivan

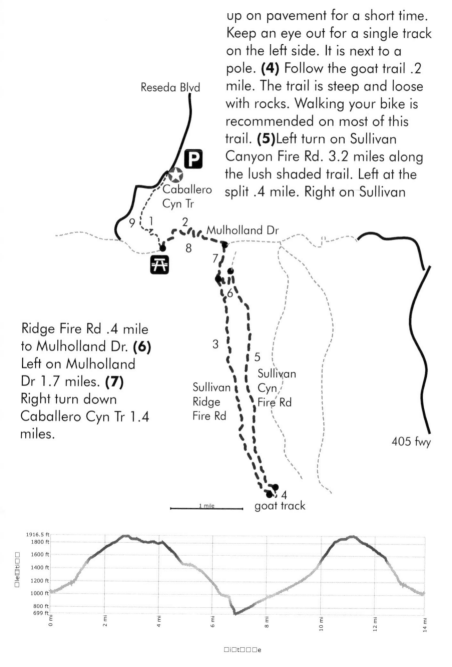

Ridge Fire Rd .4 mile to Mulholland Dr. **(6)** Left on Mulholland Dr 1.7 miles. **(7)** Right turn down Caballero Cyn Tr 1.4 miles.

Upper Las Virgenes Open Space

Santa Moncia Mountains Zone Parkland
Mountains Recreation and Conservation Authority

Nestled in Simi Hills, Upper Las Virgenes Open Space Preserve sits in between West Hills to the east and Cheeseboro Canyon to the west. The controversial, newly acquired 2,983 acres of open space (Ahmanson Ranch) purchased in 2003 is included in the 5,633 total acres of beautiful parkland. The fire roads are surrounded by beautiful oak trees, mesas, and open grassy rolling hills. The trails are mostly fire roads with gradual hills and turns. The trails are smooth, except after heavy rains when ruts can develop. This area is perfect for mountain bikers of all abilities, hikers, horseback riders, and family trips. Weekends and holidays attract many hikers and a few mountain bikers and equestrians.

Parking for Upper Las Virgenes Open Space Preserve can be accessed by three trailheads. The main trailhead located at the western end of Victory Blvd in West Hills offers a large dirt parking lot with designated trailer parking areas for a fee of $1. This trailhead is recommended for horse trailers. Ammenities include a porta potty and a couple of picnic tables. The trailhead at the northern end of Las Virgenes Canyon Rd is in Calabasas with street parking on Las Virgenes Canyon Rd approximately 2 miles north of the 101 Freeway. The parking is across the street from condominiums so parking can be limited. There is another trailhead north of Victory at the end of Vanowen St in West Hills at El Escorpion Park.

Laskey Mesa Loop

Highlights: Fire roads; rolling grassy hillsides; views; family trail; firm, smooth footing; moderate grade

Miles: 8 miles

Elevation: 850 ft

Estimated time: biking: 1-1.5 hrs
hiking and horseback riding: 2-2.5 hrs

Technical: ★★☆☆☆

Aerobic: ★★⯪☆☆

Restrooms: porta potty

Water: no

Dogs: on leash

Parking: parking lot is $1

Directions to Trailhead: GPS 34.185589,-118.668576
Upper Las Virgenes Open Space, Victory Blvd, West Hills
101 Fwy north: exit 29 toward Mulholland Dr/Valley Circle Blvd far left onto calabasas Rd. Left on Valley Circle Blvd 2 miles. Left on Victory Blvd .5 mile to the end of the road.
101 Fwy south: exit 29 for Valley Circle Blvd toward Mulholland Dr. Right on Valley Circle Blvd 2 miles. Left on Victory Blvd .5 mile to the end of the road.
This trail can also be accessed from Las Virgenes Rd in Calabasas.
*Elevation and mileage are approximate.

Overview: The trails are non-technical, wide-open fire roads with full sun exposure spotted with oak trees. The grade is moderate

E Las Virgenes Cyn Tr

Laskey Mesa Loop

with firm, smooth footing. The route is good for hiking, mountain biking, and horseback riding. From the picturesque setting at the park entrance, the trail begins on the south side of the park. **(1)** Cross the stepover and continue on the E Las Virgenes Cyn Tr .1 mile. **(2)** Left at the junction on Ahmanson Ranch House Tr as it skirts along the east side of the park for 1 mile. For a short time, there are houses to the east and grassy meadows to the west. **(3)** Right (west) on Mary Weisbrook Loop Tr .6 mile. The mesas, grassy hillsides, and wildflowers in the spring offer many lovely view points. There aren't any houses in sight for the rest of the route. **(4)** Right on Laskey Mesa Tr .8 mile descending down the canyon **(5)** Left on E Las Virgenes Cyn Tr 1.6 miles. **(6)** Right (north) on Las Virgenes Cyn Tr 1 mile. There are two water crossings on the Las Virgenes Cyn Tr; one of them is wide and there is a little mud on the side to go through; the other water crossing has a trail going around the mud with a little mud crossing. **(7)** Right on the trail .5 mile up a steep hill. **(8)** Right at the next junction for .6 mile descending to E Las Virgenes Cyn Tr. **(9)** Left on E Las Virgenes Cyn Tr 1.8 miles moderately climbing back to the parking lot.

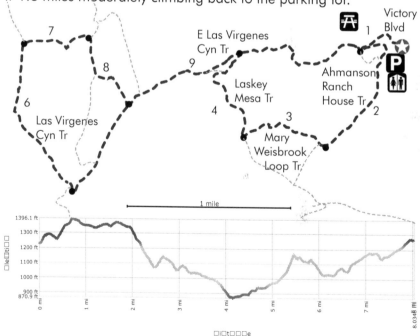

Las Virgenes Canyon Trail to Sheep Corral Trail 🚴 🥾 🐎

Highlights:	Beautiful technical single track trails with lush coastal sage scrub vegetation
Miles:	9.2
Elevation:	1050 ft
Estimated time:	biking: 1-1.5 hrs
	hiking and horseback riding: 2-3 hrs
Technical:	★★★★☆
Aerobic:	★★★☆☆
Restrooms:	no
Water:	no
Dogs:	on leash
Parking:	street parking is free

Directions to Trailhead: GPS 34.168685,-118.703488
Las Virgenes Rd, Calabasas
101 Fwy: Exit Las Virgenes Rd. North on Las Virgenes Rd 1.5 miles. The trailhead is at the end of the street.
*Elevation and mileage are approximate.

Overview: This is a very popular mountain biking trail. The footing ranges from firm smooth ground, loose rocks, uneven terrain to sandy patches. The grade is moderate. This route can also be accessed from Cheeseboro Cyn Tr in Agoura Hills/Cheeseboro Canyon. **(1)** The trail begins at the end of Las Virgenes Rd on a scenic flat fire road north along the valley floor .3 mile to an intersection. **(2)** Left at the intersection .6 mile. Pass through a water section and continue on a flat trail. **(3)** Just past the power station, left on Las Virgenes Connector Tr uphill .6 mile. This trail continues as Cheeseboro Ridge Connector heading downhill .5 mile. **(4)** Take the next trail to the right, Cheeseboro Cyn Tr. The trail begins as a shaded fire road 1.4 miles and turns into a single track 1.3 miles. The trail is lined with coastal sage scrub and wildflowers as it runs along the valley floor. You'll pass through Sulphur Springs, climb a couple technical boulder sections, and gradually ascend to Sheperd's Flat. **(5)** Head east (right) on Sheep Corral single track 2 miles downhill with ruts, drop offs, and loose dirt in areas. **(6)** Right on Upper Las Virgenes Cyn Tr 2.4 miles on a flat trail. Upper Las Virgenes Tr begins as a single track with lush vegetation and

Cheeseboro Cyn Tr

Las Virgenes Canyon Trail to Sheep Corral Trail

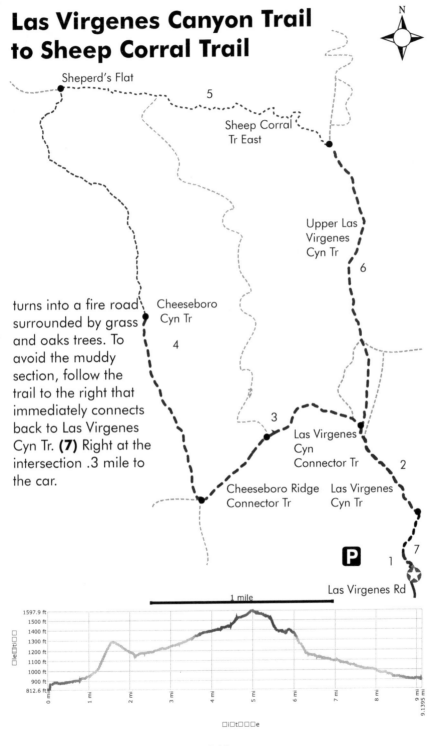

Sheperd's Flat

5

Sheep Corral
Tr East

Upper Las
Virgenes
Cyn Tr

6

turns into a fire road
surrounded by grass
and oaks trees. To
avoid the muddy
section, follow the
trail to the right that
immediately connects
back to Las Virgenes
Cyn Tr. **(7)** Right at the
intersection .3 mile to
the car.

Cheeseboro
Cyn Tr

4

3

Las Virgenes
Cyn
Connector Tr

2

Cheeseboro Ridge
Connector Tr

Las Virgenes
Cyn Tr

P 1 7

Las Virgenes Rd

1 mile

Triunfo Creek Park

Santa Moncia Mountains Zone Parkland

Triunfo Creek Park is located in the Santa Monica Mountains of Westlake Village. The area encompasses 600 acres of native grasslands, chaparral, oak woodlands, and the Pentachaeta flower. This flower is an endangered flower found in the park. The yellow flower is found only in Southern California and blooms from April to June. The Pentachaeta Trail is named after the flower. The Westlake Vista Trail is a steep, rocky trail that leads to the reservoir. The views are spectacular if you climb above the reservoir. Parking is on the side of the road. There is a cul de sac with adequate room to turn a trailer around. There aren't restrooms or water available.

Triunfo Creek Park

Highlights:	Two trails; one trail meadering to Triunfo Dr; and a trail climbing to the reservoir
Miles:	4 miles
Elevation:	750 ft
Estimated time:	biking: 1 hr
	hiking and horseback riding: 1-1.5 hrs
Technical:	★★★★☆
Aerobic:	★★★☆☆
Restrooms:	no
Water:	no
Dogs:	on leash
Parking:	street parking is free

Directions to Trailhead: GPS 34.131018,-118.821487
Triunfo Canyon Rd, Westlake Village
101 Fwy: exit 39 for Lindero Cyn Rd. South on Lindero Cyn Rd 1.6 miles. Left on Triunfo Cyn Rd 300 ft. The street dead ends at the trailhead. *Elevation and mileage are approximate.

Overview: This is a pleasant area. The Pentachaeta Trail is good for mountain biking, hiking and horseback riding. It is an intermediate trail with a moderate grade, with loose and embedded rocks. This trail leads from Lindero Cyn Rd to Triunfo Cyn Rd. Westlake Vista Trail begins gradually and quickly ascends up a

View from above the reservoir

Triunfo Creek Park

steep rocky hill leading to the reservoir. This trail seems best for hiking and horseback riding. **(1)** Begin on the Pentachaeta Tr east 1.4 miles. The trail follows houses for a short time leading to a nice shady trail with coastal sage scrub and chaparral. When the trail splits, stay to the right to go to Triunfo Cyn Rd or turn around for a return trip. **(2)** When you are back to where you started, follow the Westlake Vista Tr south uphill. The trail is rocky and steep. You will pass a trail to the right; stay straight up the hill. **(3)** At the split, turn right up a steep rocky hill .1 mile. **(4)** At the top of the hill turn right along the flat trail heading towards the reservoir .2 mile. **(5)** To return, turn around .1 mile. **(6)** Left on the first trail down the steep rocky hill .2 mile. At the junction stay straight to the trailhead.

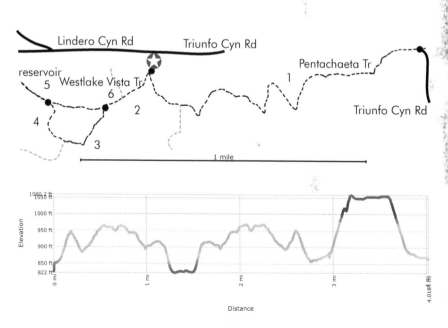

Kelly riding her horse
at the beach

Kelly riding her bike
in the hills

About the Author

Growing up, Kelly spent her weekends in a small house on Mulholland Highway. She and her sister called it the "log cabin." Before sunrise, they would cross Mulholland Hwy, go through a creek and hike the remainder of the time with wet feet. They emulated "Little House on the Prairie." Little did they know they were actually hiking near the filming of the TV show. They didn't go very far on their adventures, but it seemed like hours. As soon as the sun came out, they would sit with their toes in the sun trying to warm them, thinking they would get frostbite like people do in the movies. Kelly still enjoys the trails and uses them more than ever, but now she tries to keep her feet dry.

Every morning Kelly hikes, horseback rides, or mountain bikes the trails. She doesn't like to do the same trail two days in a row, so she is always exploring new trails. She has found herself sharing trails with friends that have lived here for over 30 years. Kelly realized there was a void of information. Her goal is to share the trails she has explored giving descriptions of each allowing you to make the best choice as to which trail best suits your needs. She tracked her rides with a GPS and cyclometer, and a thousand miles later she finished the Local Multi-Use Trail Book.

Made in the USA
San Bernardino, CA
06 June 2017